98 Days of Wind

98 Days of Wind

The Greatest Fail of Our Life

By Ras and Kathy Vaughan

Copyright © 2018 UltraPedestrian.com. All rights reserved.
Published by UltraPedestrian.com
ISBN 978-1-387-60205-6
10 9 8 7 6 5 4 3 2 1

Made Possible By

Contents

AUTHORS' NOTE 1

THE BEAUTY OF THE FAIL 3

THE ORIGINS OF BIG, CRAZY IDEAS 9

The First Yo 17

    ENTERING ARAVAIPA CANYON FOR THE FIRST TIME 34

    A CHANCE ENCOUNTER WITH ANDY RHODES 44

    ALBUQUERQUE: BOUNCE POINT ACHIEVED 89

The Final Yo 97

    LEMITAR, LOVINGKINDNESS, AND LEANING ON INNER STRENGTH 109

    WASH WALKING 114

    THE MYSTERIOUS MONTICELLO ROCK 116

    ELK 122

    GILA RIVER WILDERNESS: STORMS, SUNY, AND THE CALL OF THE GRAY WOLF 128

Epilogue: The Grand Enchantment Fail, A Diagnoses, and Life Beyond 153

    APPENDIX 1: MAGDALENA MAY, MORE THAN WORTH HER WEIGHT 161

    APPENDIX 2: GEAR LISTS 165

    ACKNOWLEDGMENTS 169

    RESOURCES 171

Authors' Note

This book is a collection of the trail dispatches and video updates (in transcript form) which we posted to the internet during our Grand Enchantment Trail Yo-yo Only Known Time project. It also includes excerpts from Kathy's personal journals kept during the adventure, as well as a few short narrative pieces written from those detailed journals. The contents of this book originally appeared as social media posts, YouTube videos, and blog articles.

To the greatest extent possible, the goal of this work is to compile and present the thoughts, ideas, and feelings generated by our experiences on the trail in their immediate, raw form. This is not intended to be a smooth, polished, mentally-metabolized version of events, with all the benefits of hindsight, rationalization, and confabulation.

This account is intended to afford the reader the opportunity to immerse themselves in the Grand Enchantment Trail and our experience of it from beginning to end, from the excitement of the preparation to the heartbreak of the aftermath.

It is our hope that, in reading this account, the reader sees us not as exceptional athletes or extraordinary specimens of any sort, but rather, as ordinary Human Beings. Because ordinary Human Beings are capable of amazing and extraordinary things.

Ras & Kathy Vaughan, May 2018

Coupeville, Washington

The Beauty of The Fail
Ninety-Eight Days All for Naught

ON JUNE 11TH, 2017, TEAM ULTRAPEDESTRIAN ACHIEVED the biggest fail of our careers. After 98 days and 1300 miles on the trail pushing our minds, bodies, gear, finances, and relationship far past their limits, we were forced to admit that we would not be able to complete our goal of becoming the first people ever to yo-yo the Grand Enchantment Trail. (Yo-yoing a trail means traveling it from one end to the other and then back again, thus completing the trail twice in a single push, once in each direction, like a yo-yo running out to the end of its string then returning to your hand.)

The GET runs east and west between Phoenix, Arizona, and Albuquerque, New Mexico, for approximately 770 miles. But the GET isn't an official trail: it's a route that links together existing trail, unmaintained trail, double-track, roads, bushwhacks, and cross-country sections that traverse both vast deserts and vertiginous mountain ranges. It's an incredibly difficult and indelibly rewarding route. Being in the heart of the American Southwest, the Grand Enchantment Trail presents a very limited window of opportunity in the spring and fall, between the freezing snows of winter and the blistering heat of summer. On our final day on the trail, when Kathy inadvertently left her sleeping pad in the direct sun and it melted, we knew that our window of opportunity had slammed shut.

Our GET Yo-yo attempt was the second in a series of four desert trail yo-yos that we planned as part of our multi-year Desert Yo-yo Grand Slam project. This included the Arizona National Scenic Trail, which we had successfully yo-yoed between September 18th and December 20th of 2015, the Grand Enchantment Trail, the Oregon Desert Trail, and the Hayduke Trail. Each of these trails is approximately 800 miles long in a single direction, and traverses some of the most challenging and unforgiving terrain in North America. We were attempting them in order of ascending difficulty, and we were under no illusion that our success was a given. These are extremely challenging routes, and there's good reason why no one had ever yo-yoed any of them before.

Not only did we aspire to being the first, but we planned to do it in "Feet On The Ground" style, not hitchhiking into resupply towns, not accepting rides of any kind, and not using public transportation or any other form of conveyance (we even avoided elevators in motels). Our goal was to cover every step of the way under our own power and on our own two feet. In or minds this would be the highest ethic we could attain, the best style, the fairest means, but it could also be summed up rather simply as, "cray cray is as cray cray does". We had invested months evaluating the physical, mental and logistical challenges involved in the overall project and had concluded that it was indeed Humanly possible. We wanted to find out if we were the Humans to do it.

When Kathy and I realized that the tide was turning against us, we knew it was more than just this one project that was on the line. We had announced our Desert Yo-yo Grand Slam project all across the state of Arizona during a speaking tour in February of 2016 and had called our shot on the interwebs for all the world to see. We had pitched proposals to sponsors to garner the support necessary to make it happen and had signed contracts promising results. We had put everything on the line, personally and professionally, for all the world to see, and now it was all crashing down around our ears.

Agonizing Decisions and Cosmic Confirmation

Kathy and I had seen the end coming, and it didn't necessarily catch us by surprise. It could even be argued that failure was the most likely outcome from the start. Our progress had been slower than we had hoped from the very beginning, and the weather never cut us even the slightest bit of slack. We began in triple digit weather and ended in triple digit weather, but the time in between was filled with postholing through knee deep snow, sheltering in culverts to wait our blizzards, hundreds of icy creek fords, painfully cold fingers and toes, and wind, wind, wind. I'm sure Mother Nature had other elemental forces with which she could have confronted us, but I'd be hard pressed to name them off the top of my head.

By day 98 Kathy had lost a drastic amount of weight and was suffering an unslakable thirst which no amount of water or other beverages was sufficient to quench. Kathy had 40% of her pancreas removed ten years ago due to a tumor, so she is even more susceptible to dehydration than the average person would be even under normal circumstances, let alone when living in and moving through the arid deserts and mountains of the Southwest for nearly 100 days. This adventure took a heavy toll on her physically, and on both of us mentally, as we watched our goals slipping further and further into the future while we struggled to cover ground.

We were constantly evaluating our progress and adjusting our plans accordingly, and yet, slowly but surely the math turned against us. Our goal of 70 days had been backed off to 80 days fairly early on. Then, 80 days was bumped back to 90. Once 100 days became our target not only was the math becoming bleak, but the weather was as well. We couldn't keep stretching out our finish date because we could feel the hot breath on our necks from the impending maw of summer.

Finally, we had the discussion that we had hoped never to have; at what point we would have to call it quits, and whether that time was now. As we neared the mining town of Morenci, there was the opportunity to bail out before committing to another multiple day stretch of blistering heat before the next chance to drop from the trail. We devised a couple of if/then statements and litmus tests to apply over the next twenty-four hours and agreed that if they didn't go the way we needed them to, we would make the call we didn't want to make. And it didn't go. The next day and night were brutally difficult, and we were both additionally burdened with the tension of sensing our impending failure. We hiked through the night to maximize movement in the cool hours, but then couldn't find proper shade deep and cool enough to rest in. Then, Kathy's sleeping pad melted. Then we sat in Eagle creek and talked out the horrible reality of choosing our well-being and health over the drive to stubbornly soldier on. We cried and hugged and held hands as we sat in the water, that being the only tenable place to wait out the heat of the day. A friend had messaged us to say he and his son would be surprising us along the route that evening, and we decided that instead of simply thanking them for their kindness, we would ask for a ride back to Phoenix.

As fate would have it, that tortuous decision had been entirely unnecessary, and our agonizing over whether or not to give up was all in vain. Wildfires sparked by lightning in the Pinaleño Mountains had closed a key section of trail, and, as it would turn out, would not be extinguished for weeks. Our Grand Enchantment Trail Yo-yo attempt would have come to an end regardless of what we had decided earlier that day. We thought we were making a decision, but, in fact, the Universe had already decided for us.

Embracing The Fail and The Un-necessity Of Proffered Solace

Neither Kathy nor I consider ourselves extraordinary athletes in any way. Our UltraPedestrian ethic promotes not what superlatively trained and supremely talented athletes can achieve, but the amazing and extraordinary things of which ordinary Human Beings are capable. (While the immediately obvious meaning of UltraPedestrian would be, "covering distances greater than that of a standard marathon on foot," an ancillary interpretation could be, "exceedingly commonplace".) Whether it be ultrarunning, fastpacking, thru-hiking, mountaineering or some agglomeration thereof, our quest is to explore the boundaries of Human endurance. Our goal is to find The Thing That We Cannot Do. In a sense, failure is our highest aim. Ticking off doable adventure after doable adventure doesn't capture our imaginations, doesn't cause our hearts sing, doesn't make our blood thrum in our ears. Guaranteed success is just a training run for the kinds of challenges that truly engage us on a deep and resonant level. The question marks are the entire point of our adventures, not just punctuation.

While I'm as impressed with and inspired by the accomplishments of elite athletes as anyone, I've long understood that their best performances are beyond the ken of the vast majority of bipeds. Our lives are the accumulation of the stories we live, and, "I had a great day, everything went perfectly, and I won," is neither a very engaging, nor a very resonant story. Challenges, struggles and perseverance through adversity are the key ingredients of the Hero's Quest. It's the relating of weaknesses, foibles, and stumblings to which the mass of Humankind can relate, and it's exactly those moments, when everything seems to be going wrong, wherein one most completely experiences his or her Humanity.

That's why I love the word fail. That's also why Kathy and I have made it part of our value set to be open and public, and even explicit with our failures. It's not a matter of self-denigration or melancholic brooding or self-flagellation, nor is it fishing for comfort or compliments. It's because the fails are where the Humanity is, and experiencing and connecting with our fundamental Humanity is the goal of adventuring, as we see it.

A Winningly Epic Fail

Our GET Yo-yo attempt was a fail of grand proportions and in full view of the public. It was a belly flop off an Olympic high dive with the gold medal on the line. It was Vinko Bogataj's cataclysmic ski jump wipeout in the opening sequence of ABC's Wide World of Sports as Jim McKay intoned, "… and the agony of defeat." It was a failure so big that it negated our previous AZT Yo-yo completion, took our planned ODT and HDT Yo-yo projects off the table, and nullified the multi-year Desert Yo-yo Grand Slam project we had been brainstorming, planning, and working toward for more than two years. Failing our Grand Enchantment Trail Yo-yo attempt was the biggest, most brutal, most beautiful, and most wonderful adventure Kathy and I have ever undertaken together. With fails as epic and rewarding as this, who needs a win?

Ras Vaughan, September 2017

Bergville, KwaZulu-Natal, South Africa

The Origins of Big, Crazy Ideas

WHILE IN THE MIDST OF AN INTENSE, 1,600+ mile double thru-hike of the Arizona National Scenic Trail, my husband of 20 years, Ras, said he had a crazy idea. He said it as if we weren't already in the middle of just such a thing. As we were making our way through the challenging and beautiful topography of the AZT, he had realized there were three other desert trails in the U.S. that are also approximately 800 miles

 Ras Vaughan is with Kathy Vaughan.
February 3, 2017

WE JUST ORDERED 40 LBS OF DEHYDRATED REFRIED BEANS, 60 lbs of dehydrated vegetarian chili, 4 lbs dehydrated mixed vegetables, 10 lbs dehydrated potato shreds, 20 lbs of wasabi peas, 8 lbs of peanut butter powder, 24 lbs of soy curls, 20 lbs of instant hummus, 58 oz tomato powder, 1.75 lbs instant organic coffee, and I'm still sourcing rice and pasta. Yep, Kathy and I have cooked up another adventure that we'll be embarking on at the end of the month. But even with all the excitement and swirling possibilities of an impending Only Known Time attempt running through my mind, I can help but wonder what sort of havoc Amazon's algorithms are going to wreak with my purchase data ... "Customers who bought this item also bought 20 lbs of instant hummus."

Special thanks to NATHAN and Altra Running for making our upcoming adventure possible.

#GETyoyo #RunLonger #ZeroLimits
#BeTrailReady #HShive #Team7hills

Ras Vaughan
February 19, 2017 · Instagram

AN IMPENDING ADVENTURE ALWAYS BEGINS TO FEEL REAL WHEN IT'S TIME TO START DEHYDRATING SOY STRIPS. These have consistently been our favorite trail food for the last few years. We season them up a few different ways (today's batches were Savory Mesquite and Lemon Pepper) then dehydrate them. On the trail we add them into rice and refried beans or chili, or minimally rehydrate them to enjoy as vegan jerky, or even just crunch on them as is. High fiber (antioxidant) and high protein (muscle repair) make them an ideal addition to our trail larder, and will help fuel us from Phoenix to Albuquerque and back.
Give Thanks for Life!

Special thanks to NATHAN and Altra Running running for making our upcoming adventure possible.

#GETyoyo #RunLonger #ZeroLimits
#BeTrailReady #HShive #Team7hills

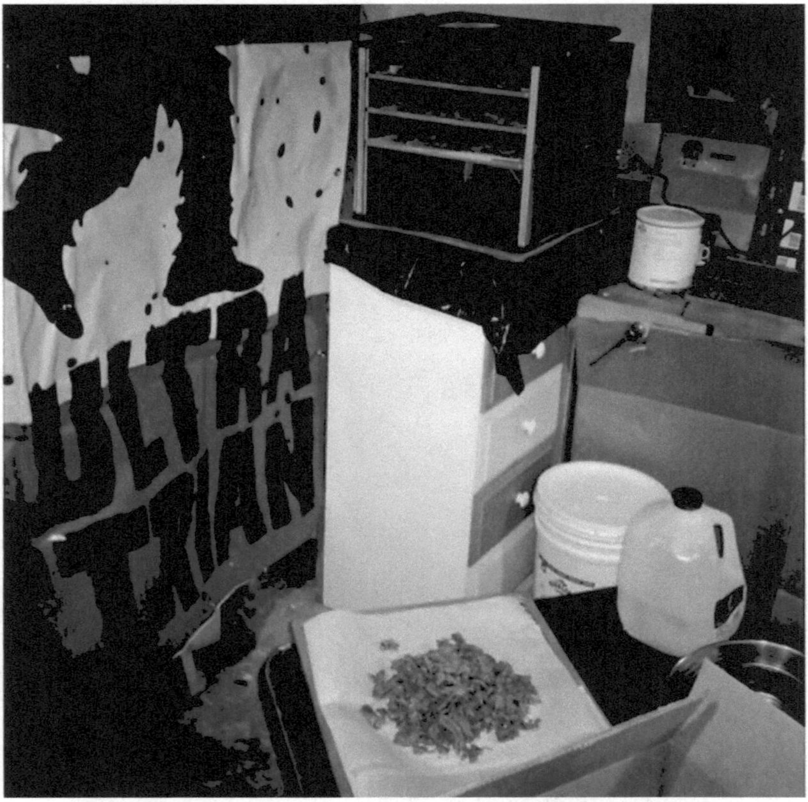

long, and that no one had attempted to yo-yo. He said this could essentially become a Desert Yo-yo Grand Slam Only Known Time project, playing out over a number of years. We were in the midst of doing something incredibly difficult that no one had ever done before, and here he was laying an even bigger, harder never-before-done idea at my feet, like a proud cat with a ravaged rodent. Unbeknownst to me, this idea had already taken on a life of its own in his mind, and we were indeed doing this.

Attempting to yo-yo another difficult desert route, let alone three more of them, sounded ludicrous to me at the time. Now, almost a year and a half later, Ras and I are gearing up for phase two of the Desert Yo-yo Grand Slam series, the 770 mile Grand Enchantment Trail. We begin the hike on March 4th (as in the command, 'March Forth!'). The trail will take us from the outskirts of Phoenix, Arizona to the mountains high above Albuquerque, New Mexico, and back again. We plan to adhere to a strict "feet on the ground" thru-hiker style attempt, meaning we will not hitchhike or accept rides into or out of towns to pick up our resupplies. We will cover every mile on our own two feet, and not set foot in a vehicle from the time we leave Phoenix until the time we return there, victorious. We will accept "trail magic" along the way (unplanned and unsolicited generosity from supporters), but will not have anyone crewing us or meeting us at pre-planned points with support of any kind, emotional or material. Our goal is to accomplish our quest according to a pure Self-Supported ethic.

Most of the projects that Ras and I do together are conceived while already engaged in another one. It makes sense. We are in our element. We are feeling high on life and endorphins. The fresh air and the natural world are filling us up with all the nourishment and sustenance we can handle, both mental and physical. We don't want to be anywhere else. We have to plan our next adventure to ensure this. This is how it works. Big, Crazy Ideas beget other Big, Crazy Ideas.

Now, just a few days before we hit the trail, Ras and I are busy putting together our twenty-one resupply packages. They are filled to the brim with dehydrated veggie chili & refried beans; rice & potatoes; dried fruits & veggies; dried marinara powder & rice noodles; hummus mix & peanut powder; wasabi peas, chocolate covered espresso beans, and dried soy curls seasoned in a variety of different ways by both Ras and I; oatmeal packets, Honey Stinger Waffles, Expedition Espresso Trail Butter, coffee, hot

Ras Vaughan is with Kathy Vaughan.
February 27, 2017

FINAL PREPARATIONS ARE UNDER WAY FOR OUR NEXT ONLY KNOWN TIME PROJECT: a yo-yo of the Grand Enchantment Trail.

Kathy's been working on our resupply boxes for almost two days straight, I'm downloading maps and GPS tracks and water data, we're both rounding up gear which is in assorted bags and bins from recent adventures, and everything is finally coming together. We've had a few setbacks over the last 18 months or so as we tried to get this project moving, but now it finally has enough momentum that it is taking off on its own. We'd especially like to thank NATHAN and Altra Running for coming through with crucial support to make it all possible. We'd also like to thank Gossamer Gear, Trail Butter, Honey Stinger, and Seven Hills Running Shop for providing fuel and gear to get us out on the trail and help keep us there.

In a day or two we'll be heading to Phoenix, AZ to begin the second phase of our Desert Yo-yo Grand Slam: hiking from Phoenix, AZ, to Albuquerque, NM, then turning around and hiking back to Phoenix, AZ. Phase One was our AZT Yo-yo in the fall of 2015. At this point we've been in civilization far too long, and we're ready to get back to the Real World and the beautiful and challenging environs of the deserts and mountains!

What a Blessing to be a Hominid!

#GETyoyo #GETit #ZeroLimits #RunLonger #TakeLessDoMore #BeTrailReady #Team7Hills #HShive

chocolate, tea, and soups. We have everything we need to fuel the 1,500+ miles we will hike together through Arizona and New Mexico. Putting together these resupply boxes is both daunting and exhilarating. Late last night, Ras was taping together bundles of batteries for our headlamps, loading up our new Mp3 players and making sure we had all the trail beta. I looked at him with my eyes glazed over and said, "I still need to bake chocolate chip banana muffins for the road and get my blog posted from my Methow Trails 200k Ski Challenge in January." Ah, the life of an adventurer. I would only trade it for a life filled with more adventuring.

Ras Vaughan
March 4, 2017 · Coupeville

HERE'S A PEAK BEHIND THE SCENES AT ALL OF OUR RESUPPLY BOXES right before we hauled them to the post office. You get a very different idea of your food choices and caloric intake when you package up two or three months worth of food and pack it into boxes! Plus, more philosophical blithering and gear dorking!
What a Blessing to be a Hominid!

#GETyoyo #GETit #GrandEnchantmentTrail #ZeroLimits #RunLonger #TakeLessDoMore #BeTrailReady #Team7hills #HShive

GET Yo-yo Attempt In Altra Zero Drop Footwear
Ras and Kathy are attempting the first known yo-yo of the...
YOUTUBE.COM

Our old dog Puzzle and our furry, loveable cat Dodger will stay behind with Ras' mother. Our belongings will be safe and protected in a storage unit, and the guest room of Ras' mother's home. Our ultrarunner friend Miguel Moreno, owner of The UltraHouse in Phoenix, will keep our car at his place while we trek to the far reaches of New Mexico and back again to Arizona. My mother will ship our boxes to us for the westbound portion of our hike. An anonymous donor helped us with a few final pieces of important gear. Other friends have offered to meet us on the trail with a warm hello, water, and encouragement. An adventure of this magnitude becomes easier with the support of our surrounding community. Ras and I are both grateful for this, knowing that others have helped make a thru-hike of the Grand Enchantment Trail possible for us.

Ras Vaughan is with Kathy Vaughan.
March 2, 2017 · Instagram

WE'LL MISS YOU, WASHINGTON! But, alas, Arizona and New Mexico are calling, and adventure awaits! Fret not, though, you still have a firm hold on our hearts and minds, and there are still challenges aplenty to lure us home to you, WA.
What a Blessing to be a Pacific Northwest Hominid!

#GETyoyo #GETit #GrandEnchantmentTrail
#ZeroLimits #RunLonger #TakeLessDoMore #BeTrailReady #Team7hills
#HShive

After returning from our last thru-hike yo-yo of the Arizona Trail, we worked for fifteen months for a yard care and weeding service to wrap up expenses from that hike and prepare to set out on the trail again for this GET thru-hike yo-yo. Determined to get back out on the trail, we accepted side jobs and sent in proposals for sponsorship funding. Gossamer Gear, Seven Hills Running Shop in Seattle, Honey Stinger and Bogg's Trail Butter all came through with generous amounts of gear and trail nutrition. Altra Running partnered up with Nathan Sports to provide the crucial support necessary to make this adventure possible, and in so doing made the dreams and ambitions of the second hike in our Desert Yo-yo Grand Slam project a reality. We both feel honored, supported, understood and blessed. Our goal is to inspire others to live their dreams, get outside and explore, push beyond perceived physical and mental limitations, and make spending time with those you love a priority. Zero Limits is a mentality and a philosophy we live by and want to spread to others. And thanks to the support of these companies, we have the opportunity to do just that.

Ras Vaughan
March 4, 2017

OFFICIAL ONLY KNOWN TIME ATTEMPT ANNOUNCEMENT:
The Grand Enchantment Trail is a 770 mile route that runs roughly east and west between Phoenix, AZ, and Albuquerque, NM.

Starting the afternoon of March 4th (get it, march forth?) Kathy and I, Team UltraPedestrian, will begin our attempt to be the first people to yo-yo the GET. We hope to make it in 70 days or so. We plan to adhere to a strict feet-on-the-ground ethic, self-supported, accepting no rides or hitchhiking.

You can follow our progress on our SPOT transponder at:
http://share.findmespot.com/shared/faces/viewspots.jsp...

And we will be posting updates to our Facebook, Instagram, and
https://www.instagram.com/ultrapedestrian/
https://www.youtube.com/c/ultrapedestrianchannel

https://youtu.be/AmgOnE_fsJs

#GETyoyo #GETit #GrandEnchantmentTrail #ZeroLimits #RunLonger #TakeLessDoMore #BeTrailReady #Team7hills #HShive

GET Yo-yo Attempt With Nathan Hydration
Ras and Kathy are attempting the first known yo-yo of the...
YOUTUBE.COM

Give Thanks for Life!

    Kathy Vaughan, February 2017

    Coupeville, Washington

Ras Vaughan is with Kathy Vaughan.
March 3, 2017 · Instagram

ADVENTURE #1: LOCKING OUR KEYS IN THE CAR. We made it all the way to Eagles' Landing Rest Stop south of Provo, Utah, before we pulled off to sleep for a couple of hours. Then we went into the Flying J Travel Plaza to get some morning coffee, each thinking the other had the keys. Luckily, when we couldn't find them, we realized they were safely locked in our vehicle. Fortunately for us, this is just the sort of situation in which Randy from the adjacent tire shop shines. He cheerfully slimjimmed our Suzuki Vitara open, refused to charge us, and then thanked us for the opportunity to help. We thanked him in return, and he is now the proud owner of a well earned UltraPedestrian sticker. Thanks again, Randy!
Faith in Humanity reaffirmed!
What a Blessing to be a member of a highly social species! Give Thanks for Life!

#GETyoyo #GETit #GrandEnchantmentTrail #ZeroLimits #RunLonger #TakeLessDoMore #BeTrailReady #Team7hills #HShive

The First Yo

March Forth! Day 1 3/4/17 Journal entry

We made it to the GET start! The Householder family got us to the First Water Trailhead. We started @ 7:02 p.m., typical! 7 mi.

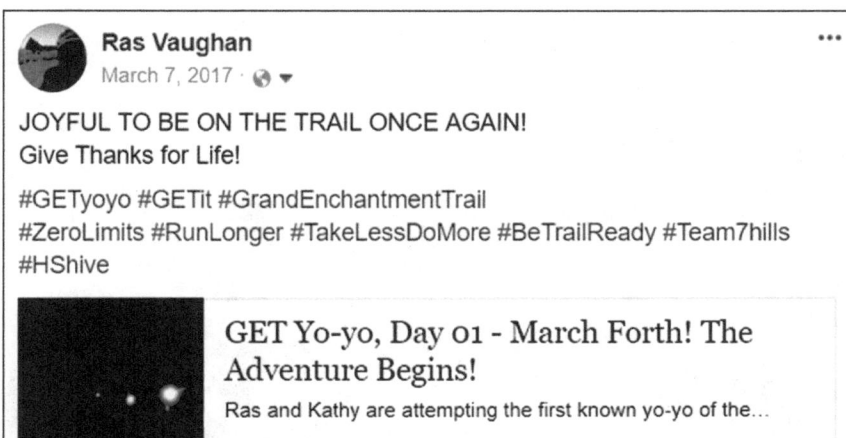

GET Yo-yo, Day 01 Video Transcript:

March Forth! The Adventure Begins!

Ras: "Yo yo! That's our greeting for the next 70 or more days. And it is 7:02 PM on March fourth (march forth!). We are officially beginning the GET yo-yo. Kind of a silly time of day to start, but we wanted to use this date because it's fun. And we're just not overly worried, and we like hiking in the dark, and this is a kind of nice way to start off. So, this is it. It is awesome indeed. So stoked to be out in the real world again."

Ras Vaughan is at Superstition Mountains.
March 6, 2017 · Instagram

GET YO-YO, DAY 02 - SAGUAROS ARE SOME OF MY FAVORITE PEOPLE. Walking among them is like moving through a giant cocktail party frozen in time. I wish I could eavesdrop on those conversations.
What a Blessing to be Alive!

#GETyoyo #GETit #GrandEnchantmentTrail #ZeroLimits #RunLonger #TakeLessDoMore #BeTrailReady #Team7hills #HShive

Ras Vaughan
March 7, 2017 · Instagram

GET YO-YO, DAY 03: Walking the wilds in wonder at the rugged beauty of Creation! This natural arch in Rogers Canyon was just one of a host of wonders, including an amazing amount of delicious water; such an especial Blessing in the desert.

#GETyoyo #GETit #GrandEnchantmentTrail
#ZeroLimits #RunLonger #TakeLessDoMore #BeTrailReady #Team7hills #HShive

Ras Vaughan is with Kathy Vaughan.
March 8, 2017 · Instagram

GET YO-YO, DAY 04: This is my favourite plant in the world. I don't mean Saguaros as a species, I mean this specific individual Saguaro. How ancient and amazing.
What a Blessing to be a Hominid!
Give Thanks for Life!

#GETyoyo #GETit #GrandEnchantmentTrail
#ZeroLimits #RunLonger #TakeLessDoMore #BeTrailReady #Team7hills #HShive

Kathy Vaughan
March 8, 2017

Back in the desert with my love; back on 70 miles of the Arizona Trail, where it doubles with the Grand Enchantment Trail. Ras and I are meandering through the varied desert landscapes and embracing the challenge, scenery, heat, abundance of food & water. The wildflowers are bright and everywhere. Life is Good. #RunLonger. #ZeroLimits. #Team7Hills #Getityoyo. #GrandEnchantmentTrail. #TakeLessDoMore. #PureNaturalEnergy. #BeTrailReady

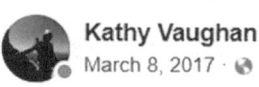

> **Ras Vaughan**
> March 10, 2017
>
> GET YO-YO, DAY 04, #1 - Sunset Outside Superior and Transitioning to Night Hiking
>
> #GETyoyo #GETit #GrandEnchantmentTrail #ZeroLimits #RunLonger #TakeLessDoMore #BeTrailReady #Team7hills #HShive
>
> https://youtu.be/tzaManUTzHE
> u
>
> **GET Yo-yo, Day 04, #1 - Progress Update Outside Superior, AZ**
> Ras and Kathy are attempting the first known yo-yo of the Grand Enchantment Trail. Day 04 finds them outside Superior, AZ, as the sun is setting and they are...
> YOUTUBE.COM

GET Yo-yo, Day 4 Video Transcript

Progress Update Outside Superior, Arizona

Ras: "We are just outside the town of Superior, Arizona. We're not resupplying there, we just happen to be near there and are taking a break as the sun sets behind us. We're making our transition into nighttime hiking. It's been fairly hot, even though we thought we were getting a pretty early start, season-wise. So, we were taking lots of breaks during the day and we're planning on making a good push and trying to get ten miles or so after dark and help round out our day. The last year and a half we've been living at sea level, and just not living as hard as we were before, and it's showing in our trail preparedness. So, we have been taking some time, not necessarily by choice, it's just taking time for us to get our trail legs and get accustomed to the heat and the elevation. So, we're off to a little bit of a slow start but we're stoked to be out here giving it a go and making our attempt on a Grand Enchantment Trail yo-yo and just being back in Arizona and the Southwest and this beautiful country that we love so much."

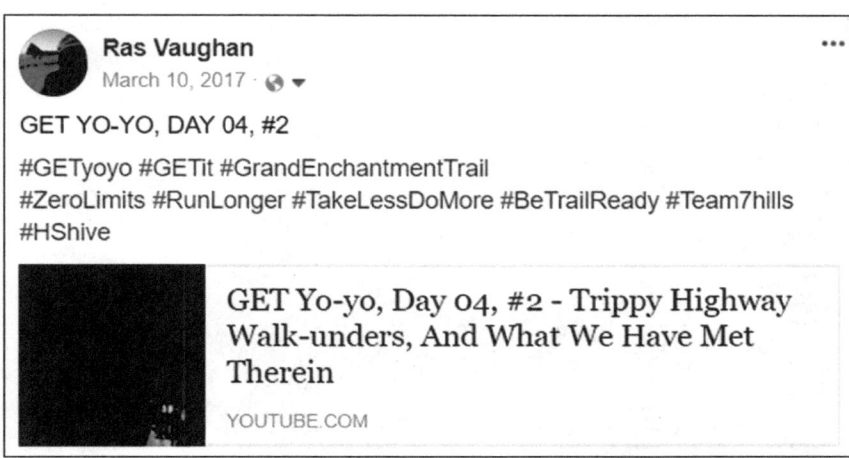

GET Yo-yo, Day 04 #2 Video Transcript

Trippy Highway Walk-unders, And What We Have Met Therein

Ras: "We're passing under the highway outside Superior. This section of the GET is part of the AZT as well. And on the AZT, at least, there's a number of these freeway walk-unders, which often have crazy or weird stuff in them. You can see a bat flying away from us, far down. One of these, a real short one we walked through, had black widow spiders all over the ceiling. Another time there were a whole bunch of flickers hanging up in the corners. So it's always a little bit of a weird experience hiking through these. But this one just had a single bat that fled before us. So, nothing too trippy."

Ras Vaughan is with Kathy Vaughan.
March 9, 2017 · Instagram

HOW EMBARRASSING!
I'm six days into a 1540+ mile double thruhike with my beloved OBAL from Phoenix to Albuquerque and back to Phoenix, and I just realized I'm wearing the exact same bandana I'll be wearing in the Fijian jungle tonight on teevee. Dang, I need to up my bandana game!

#KickingAndScreaming #OneBadAssLady #GETyoyo #GETit #GrandEnchantmentTrail
#ZeroLimits #RunLonger #TakeLessDoMore #BeTrailReady #Team7hills #HShive

> **Ras Vaughan**
> March 10, 2017
>
> GRAND ENCHANTMENT TRAIL YO-YO, DAY 06 - A Wealth of Wildflowers and Water.
> #GETyoyo #GETit #GrandEnchantmentTrail #ZeroLimits #RunLonger #TakeLessDoMore #BeTrailReady #Team7hills #HShive
>
> https://youtu.be/ZTABcAAdhVU
>
>  **GET Yo-yo, Day 06 - A Wealth of Wildflowers and Water**
> Ras and Kathy are attempting the first known yo-yo of the...
> YOUTUBE.COM

GET Yo-yo, Day 06 Video Transcript

A Wealth Of Wildflowers And Water

Kathy: "We are, right now, hiking through the Gila River canyon. And the wildflowers are in bloom; poppies and wild lupine and it's just spectacular. We're enjoying it. It's hot, but this is really a beautiful section of trail."

Ras: "And this is a section that we've done a number of times, because it's part of the AZT and the GET overlaps with it here. And it's been amazing how much water there's been compared to normal. There were a bunch of rains right before we started out. So, we've had great water the whole time for Arizona. You can see all these wild flowers that are the result of that. They're gonna be pretty short-lived. The other thing that's been enjoying the wet so much has been frogs. We've been seeing a crazy number of frogs. It's obviously their mating time, so we'll hear one frog singing out really loud. And then we'll see other frogs crossing the trail trying to get to them. And we caught a couple of frogs actually in congress, getting busy, as it were. And we've found potholes just teaming with tadpoles. So, it's amazing the life that's brought out in the desert during the brief abundant periods of water."

Ras Vaughan is in Kearny, Arizona.
March 10, 2017 · Instagram

NO TRESPASSING SIGNS ONLY APPLY TO PEOPLE WHO DON'T ASK PERMISSION. When ol' Ray pulled up next to us in his diesel pickup I simply told him we were hoping to use the old Camino Rio road to avoid walking the highway or the railroad tracks from Kearny back to Kelvin. I asked him if we could hike across his ranch and he readily gave his assent. We thanked him and shook hands. As we were walking through we watched him herd an errant horse back into a pen with his truck, and his hands asked us if we had enough water and warned us about the snakes being out. Very friendly shortcut. I always seem to get along just fine with country people, regardless of larger societal stereotypes.
Give Thanks for Life!

#GETyoyo #GETit #GrandEnchantmentTrail
#ZeroLimits #RunLonger #TakeLessDoMore #BeTrailReady #Team7hills #HShive

The Greatest Fail of Our Life

Ras Vaughan is with Kathy Vaughan.
March 11, 2017 · Instagram

GET YO-YO, DAY 08
The best Life isn't one where you sip champagne, but one where you guzzle water.

#HominidUp #OneBadAssLady #GETyoyo #GETit #GrandEnchantmentTrail #ZeroLimits #RunLonger #TakeLessDoMore #BeTrailReady #Team7hills #HShive

29

Ras Vaughan
March 11, 2017 · Instagram

GET YO-YO, DAY 08: Team UltraPedestrian Midnight Moonlight selfie. I'm so Blessed to move through wild and challenging places with my Beloved OBAL.
Give Thanks for Life!

#OneBadAssLady
#GETyoyo #GETit #GrandEnchantmentTrail
#ZeroLimits #RunLonger #TakeLessDoMore #BeTrailReady #Team7hills #HShive

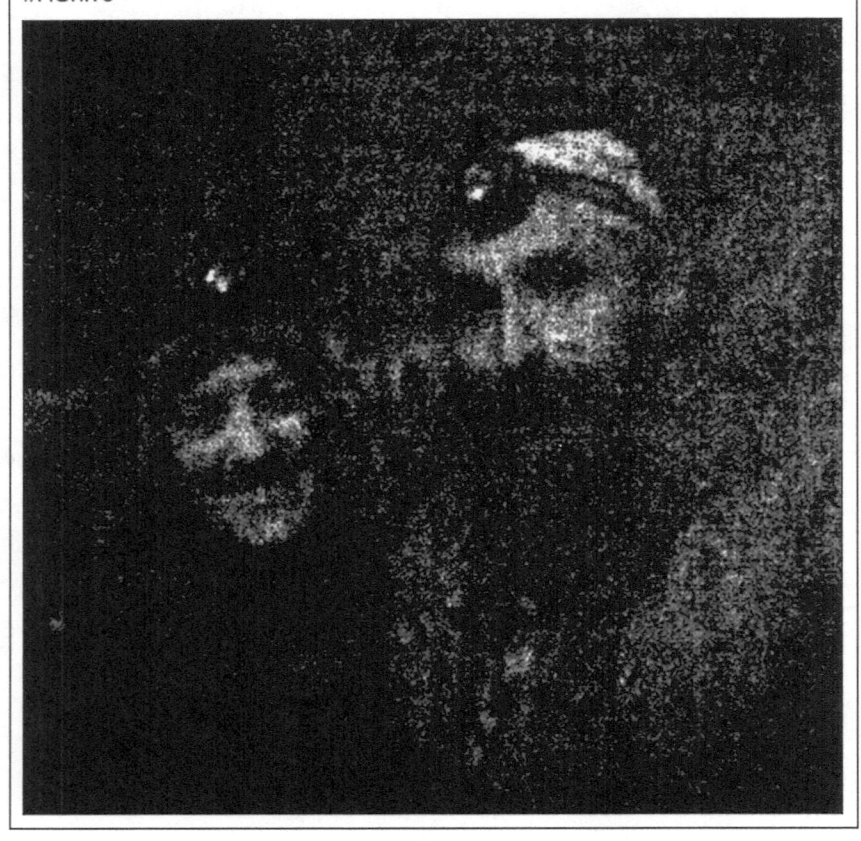

> **Ras Vaughan** is with Kathy Vaughan.
> March 13, 2017 · Instagram
>
> GET YO-YO, DAY 10: I'M PRETTY SURE 'DISTANCE LEARNING' IS PRECISELY THE PURSUIT IN WHICH WE ARE ENGAGED. I wonder if Central Arizona College offers a degree in Bipedal Studies. And, if so, I wonder if they give credit for applicable life experience. A program like that might tempt me into pursuing a higher edumuhcation!
> What a Blessing to be Hominids learning about Life, the Universe, and Everything with our own two feet!
>
> #GETyoyo #GETit #GrandEnchantmentTrail #ZeroLimits #RunLonger #TakeLessDoMore #BeTrailReady #Team7hills #HShive

Day 11 3/14/17 Journal entry

*@ Brandenburg Campsite, about to enter Aravaipa Canyon. Last night had exciting hike towards canyon. Rocky, crazy steep, route finding. Took a break at Central Arizona College-NICE, shade, water, grass, electrical outlet. No Students. "Memorizing Shadows", Ranger at Brandenburg *

> **Ras Vaughan**
> March 22, 2017 · YouTube
>
> #GETyoyo #GETit #GrandEnchantmentTrail #ZeroLimits #RunLonger #TakeLessDoMore #BeTrailReady #Team7hills #HShive
>
> **GET Yo-yo, Day 11, #1 - Entering The West End Of Aravaipa Canyon**
> Ras and Kathy are attempting the first known yo-yo of the Grand Enchantment Trail. They now head into Aravaipa Canyon, a rich riparian zone that slashes thro...
> YOUTUBE.COM

GET Yo-yo, Day 11 Video Transcript

Entering The West End Of Aravaipa Canyon

Kathy: "We've just reached Aravaipa Canyon, with a whole bunch of water, which is really awesome. We're gonna be hiking through it for the day. It's cooling us down. It's a really unique area to hike through, and we're loving it so far. We got off a three-mile dusty dirt road hike into this."

Ras: "Which is a pretty nice change of scenery with willows and cottonwoods and …"

Kathy: "Cattail!"

Ras: "Yeah, wow, cattail even. So, there's some food and fiber and other things. We've had pretty warm weather, so far, the beginning of this trip.

That might sound disingenuous since it is the desert, but this time of year would normally be a little bit cooler. We've had some kinda early warm temperatures and that has affected our trip a little bit. We've been going slower, doing a lot more sit breaks and shade breaks during the day, taking a siesta during the hottest hours from 3:00 to 5:00 or so, and then doing a lot of night hiking, which we normally do anyway. Going up until midnight or 1:00 each evening, enjoying the cool air, and moving in that uniquely quiet and solitary time of day, under cover of darkness."

Entering Aravaipa Canyon for The First Time

DAY 11 BEGAN WITH FRESH FRUIT FROM HEIDI, the ranger for the station near the west entrance to Aravaipa Canyon. She had been friendly with Ras and I in the morning, as we showed her our pass and she gave us the okay to enter the canyon. Ras had gone over to the station to get water in the morning and check into whether or not a ranger was around. They struck up a conversation, and soon she came over to our camp with a notepad to jot down any interesting information about the ultralight gear we were carrying on our hike. She brought over some fruit and told us to leave the empty container near the sign when we hit the trail. We enjoyed our visit with the first ranger we had met along the trail.

Ras and I at first welcomed the beautiful water of Aravaipa Creek, but soon tired of the sand and small rocks collecting in the bottom of our Lone Peaks, making it hard for us to hike very efficiently. We had to continually cross the creek, looking for the best route on the other side. A flood had swept through the canyon in 2006, wiping out much of the established trails. The length of the canyon is 12 miles. We had thought we would make good time hiking through here, but the collection of sediment was slowing us down. We finally stopped for a late afternoon snack and rest break, the canyon walls towering above us and the creek flowing around us on all sides. We had found a nice sand bar to set up our break spot. Ras got the stove going, and we discussed how we could use duct tape to seal off the tops of our gaiters.

Schools of small fish swam upstream in the creek. A gentle breeze blew making the leaves in the cottonwoods rustle, and birds of all varieties flitted about. Vermillion fly catchers caught my eye, and I confused them for cardinals. The scenic canyon had a very special energy, and once we sealed our shoes off from the sand and pebbles, Ras and I were drawn through this magical environment with a more gentle flow. Soon, it was dark and we stopped to have a quick cup of coffee and get out our headlamps.

A group of headlamps made their way towards us. We heard the voices too, and I speculated that the small group was just out for a nice night hike through the dark canyon. Once the hikers got to us, they asked if either of us had any first aid training. Ras answered that he had First Responder training. A lady, who appeared to be in her 60's and a competent hiker, explained that while hiking into the canyon that morning, her hiking partner had injured her ankle or foot. She wasn't sure of the extent of the injuries, but she had set her up as comfortably as possible and was recruiting help from other hikers in the canyon. She had already hiked east and gotten assistance from others along the way, and was now heading back to her friend. The lady was named Anne, and she had two other hikers with her that were helping her carry her backpack. Anne had come into the canyon that morning with an injured shoulder already. She felt like she could handle the hike, but now, after having hiked additional mileage through the canyon to help her friend, she could no longer bear the weight of the pack. Ras and I agreed to hike along with the group and Ras would evaluate Anne's friend for her, as soon as we got to where she was waiting.

I was impressed with Anne's ability to navigate through the creek and the canyon floor. She pushed her way through the creek efficiently as she sought the best way to move, finding the trail on the other side and hiking quickly until it was time to cross again. It was all so mysterious to me and I followed along, bringing up the rear. Everyone was bundled up on top but staying just a bit chilled from the water crossings. Each hiker had a different way of gearing up for the repeated fords; hiking boots, or gaiters, or running shoes. We approached a couple camped along the creek, and they joined up with us, the guy taking Anne's pack now and the other two hikers returning to their camp. It had all been worked out ahead of time, and still it felt so confusing and ethereal to me. I just took up my place again, in the rear of the pack. Ras rushed to stay up with the others, having some concern for Anne as he felt that she must be pushing forward on mostly adrenaline at this point. He reminded her to drink occasionally, and pointed out that she should have a snack too. Anne's injured friend did not have much gear with her, was on her first backpacking trip, and the extent of her injuries was unconfirmed. Ras was concerned that she might even be in a life-threatening situation.

After several hours, we finally saw a campfire ahead, and there was Anne's friend Anna, with a nice guy who had been keeping her company for many hours. He went back to his family camped a couple of miles away, and Ras set to work looking at Anna's ankle. Anne had wrapped it for her and she had it elevated. She was near the fire, alert, but still in shorts. She actually had no pack. Anne had been carrying everything with her in her backpack. It was quite an odd situation.

After evaluating the ankle, Ras determined that she could not walk out of the canyon on her own. They would need to call for rescue. They had an emergency beacon that had been borrowed from another hiker during Anne's daytime hike seeking assistance. The beacon would be seen from inside the canyon, and it was up to them whether or not they wanted to trigger it. Ras advised them that they would likely need help, but he did not want to be the one to set off the beacon. Anna asked what it would mean logistically, and we said that we thought a rescue team would come in on horseback in the morning. We helped set up the tent, I helped Anna into some warmer clothing and into her sleeping bag, and off we went. We had also exchanged contact information with Anne.

Ras and I hiked for another hour or so, and then set up a nice camp at a wider spot in the canyon where a side canyon, Hells Canyon, cuts off into the towering rock. We were pretty tired from the excitement of the night, and we were ready for some good sleep. A Ringtail spied on us from a branch overhead, and we were sure to keep a clean camp as we tucked into our tent for the night. All of a sudden, the loud and distinctive roar of helicopter propellers came echoing through the canyon. It sounded low and close. We were surprised to hear the helicopter so late at night and it didn't take long to realize that it most likely was responding to the emergency beacon. I wondered how injured Anna was and hoped that this rescue mission was legitimate, yet I did not want Anna to be seriously injured.

It was such an exhilarating moment. The helicopter seemed to see Ras and I down below, and we shut off our headlamps and just lay still. We didn't know the signal for "not us" or any way to communicate effectively with the helicopter crew. The spot light was overwhelmingly bright and the roar of the propellers was intense. We stared at each other and kept still, wondering what the heck we should do, if anything. After what seemed like an eternity, the helicopter finally stopped centering its attention on us. We listened to it fly away, searching the canyon below for the emergency beacon and the injured hiker, only a mile or so from where we lay. The sound of the searching chopper lasted for maybe 45 minutes, and then nothing, just the silence of the canyon at night and the continual ripple of the creek.

Morning came, and with it the return of the helicopter. This time, the noise of the propeller blades lasted for a much shorter duration, and Ras and I assumed that Anne and Anna had been located. An email from Anne later confirmed this assumption, the next time Ras and I were in an area where we had service. Anna and Anne had both been airlifted out of the canyon, and Anna had a spiral fracture of her tibia. Ras had made the right call in advising the ladies to request rescue, Anne was able to catch a ride out and did not have to hike out solo with her pack as she had feared, and Anna got the medical attention she needed. Our hike through Aravaipa Canyon was a little more exciting than we had planned, although we had looked forward to the journey through the canyon for many weeks.

Kathy Vaughan
March 22, 2017

Endurance challenges are tough in and of themselves. Add desert heat; thorny bushes overgrowing the trail; steep summits by way of cross country travel through snow, or rocks or desert brush; canyon tromping with creek fords; and huge stretches between resupply spots, meaning heavy packs. But the water is abundant, the Sky Island peaks are majestic and rugged, the solitude & time for mental pondering is boundless, and I wouldn't trade it for anything. I love that I am confronting new challenges on this route. Night hiking while bushwacking up steep climbs is exhilarating; fording rushing canyon creeks in the dark is thrilling; descending boulder gullies keeps you focused. Bring it! At 50, I am up for learning & experiencing even more of what life has to offer. I feel blessed. Get outside and live!
#ZeroLimits #BeTrailReady. #Team7Hills. #RunStronger. #HSHive. #TakeLessDoMore. #GETit. #GrandEnchantmentTrail

> **Ras Vaughan**
> March 22, 2017 · YouTube
>
> #GETyoyo #GETit #GrandEnchantmentTrail #ZeroLimits #RunLonger #TakeLessDoMore #BeTrailReady #Team7hills #HShive
>
> **GET Yo-yo, Day 11, #2 - The Joys Of Night Hiking In Aravaipa Canyon**
> Ras and Kathy are attempting the first known yo-yo of the...
> YOUTUBE.COM

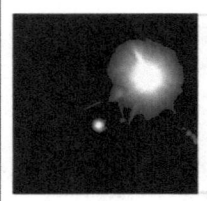

GET Yo-yo, Day 11 #2 Video Transcript

The Joys Of Night Hiking In Aravaipa Canyon

Ras: "We are still in Aravaipa Canyon, moving along slowly. It's just slow moving with winding our way back and forth across the creek in the floor of the canyon here. But it's a really amazing place to be, and it's especially amazing to get to do it after dark. Not a lot of people get to move through places like this after dark, and it's always a special sort of adventure and blessing to us. We don't get to see everything, although we can look up and see the canyon walls with our headlamps, but we also get to see things. We saw a Ringtail in a tree just a moment ago. Wouldn't have seen that during the day because it was a reflection of its eyes that caught our attention. Lots of bats. A little brown one flew really close to my face catching mosquitos in the light of my headlamp. And a bunch of frogs and some pollywogs that are pretty far along. So, just having a fun time continuing our movement through Aravaipa Canyon."

Ras Vaughan
March 20, 2017 · Instagram

GET YO-YO, DAY 13 - WANDERING THE SANTA TERESA MOUNTAINS. Lots of wash-walking, bushwhacking, and route finding in this segment made for slow going. But that's part of the fun of an Only Known Time attempt. And the goal of our yo-yo projects is to experience the trail as completely as possible, so more immersion in the environs only helps us toward our goal. What a Blessing to be a Biped!

#GETyoyo #GETit #GrandEnchantmentTrail #ZeroLimits #RunLonger #TakeLessDoMore #BeTrailReady #Team7hills #HShive

Day 15 3/18/17 Journal Entry

It was nice to get up high, into a forest cover of manzanita, ponderosa, other pine variety, juniper. The needles are soft in camp. It's quiet and solitude abounds out here. *

> **Ras Vaughan**
> March 22, 2017 · YouTube
>
> #GETyoyo #GETit #GrandEnchantmentTrail #ZeroLimits #RunLonger #TakeLessDoMore #BeTrailReady #Team7hills #HShive
>
> **GET Yo-yo, Day 15 - Blue Ribbon Scavenger Hunt: A Route, Not A Trail**
> Ras and Kathy are attempting the first known yo-yo of the Grand Enchantment Trail. The GET is a route, not an official long trail, and here Ras gives you a g...
> YOUTUBE.COM

GET Yo-yo, Day 15 Video Transcript

Blue Ribbon Scavenger Hunt: A Route, Not A Trail

Ras: "This is one of the blue ribbons. The GET, the Grand Enchantment Trail, even though it's called a trail, is actually a route. And it links together a bunch of existing trail, including parts of the Arizona National Scenic Trail, as well as a whole bunch of trail that doesn't exist all that much anymore, a bunch of unmaintained trail, some just cross-country bushwhacking overland sections and a bunch of Forest Service road and two-track, 4x4 road, Jeep road, that sort of stuff. This is actually one of the nicer sections of trail that we've been on, aside from the AZT where it's really well maintained. We're in the Pinaleños Mountains, one of the sky islands, up about 7,000 feet. You can see there's a unique combination of flora. It's always interesting to me when we're up higher in Arizona and you get the combination of pines with cacti. I'm not used to thinking of those two things living together, but there's the type of cactus we saw a moment ago, there's also prickly pear in here, and then there's Piñon Pine and we've been in some Ponderosa (I don't know about right here), and juniper of course, as well. But this is just a little taste of some of the nicer trail tread on the Grand Enchantment Trail. This whole route ends up becoming kind of like a giant scavenger hunt where you're just trying to locate the blue ribbons. Blister Free, who designed the route, has marked certain areas with ribbons. I don't know how frequently they get redone, but it's always encouraging when you see one. They're kind of like the confidence markers in an ultramarathon, in a hundred-mile race, something like that. So here all of the turns aren't necessarily marked, and some sections you could go a day without seeing a ribbon, but when you do you know you are still on the GET, whenever you see one of those blue ribbons. So that's pretty much all you gotta do: string together the ribbons."

Kathy Vaughan is with Ras Vaughan.
March 20, 2017 ·

Webb Peak- The highest point on the GET in AZ. We made it there today after some snow navigating and are now on the descent. I'm loving this crazy adventurous route!! I can' t believe what Ras and I have already hiked through. Giving thanks that I can do this; that Ras and I are seizing this blessing and that we have the support of family, friends, community and companies that believe in us. #NathanSports. #AltraRunning. #TrailButter. #HoneyStinger #Team7Hills. #GossamerGear.

> **Ras Vaughan**
> March 22, 2017 · YouTube
>
> #GETyoyo #GETit #GrandEnchantmentTrail #ZeroLimits #RunLonger #TakeLessDoMore #BeTrailReady #Team7hills #HShive
>
> ### GET Yo-yo, Day 17 - The Benefits Of Hunger Both Literal And Figurative
>
> Ras and Kathy are attempting the first known yo-yo of the Grand Enchantment Trail. After 150 miles without resupply they are approaching the town of Safford,...
>
> YOUTUBE.COM

GET Yo-yo, Day 17 Video Transcript

The Benefits Of Hunger Both Literal And Figurative

Ras: "We are just a couple miles outside of Safford, Arizona. We're stoked to be heading into town to get our resupply. Our previous resupply was at Kearny, so this was like 150 miles with no resupply over some pretty tough ground; a fair amount of cross-country off-trail travel, real challenging stuff. Yesterday in a single day we dealt with everything from postholing hip-deep in snow to crossing snowmelt-swollen streams by headlamp, fording them over and over again, to having to dodge various cacti and rattlesnake during a midnight bushwhack across the top of a mesa. So quite a variety of experiences; definitely qualifies as an adventure. We're a couple days late getting to this resupply, so we have gone through our food stores and *everything pretty hard. We have been really low on calories the last two days, and yet just having this amazing experience seeing how incredibly far our bodies can go on how little, when we are eating virtually nothing but using our fat stores for fuel. We just had our last serving of dehydrated chili this morning. We just are finishing our last drink packages. We stretched it out and everything went perfect. We're gonna hit a minimart in just a couple minutes here and have a couple of treats. And, Kathy, you had an experience with strawberry powder ..."*

Kathy: *"Yes. Our friend Gary Householder gave us some dehydrated fruit when he met us with some water and some yummy food from a vegan café. It was so kind. He had packets of dehydrated strawberries and dehydrated apples, and we mixed them together into a ziplock and I just savored them. They started disintegrating into powder, and I would take little pinches of the fruit out and share it with Ras, and this morning that was what I had left. I finished it off, poured it in my water bottle. I've got one that's got my Trail Butter sticker on it for flavored drinks, like electrolyte drinks or Emergen-C, and that's what it has in it right now, strawberry powder and one last Emergen-C that Ras had saved for me. It's the little things that count. It's what's getting us this seven-mile hike. We've been hiking from that mountain range all down this road to get into town for our resupply box and some other food."*

Ras: *"We're about to have a little taste of civilization which we will enjoy, but we also know from past experience we'll tire of rather quickly. So, we'll be back on the trail with full bellies and full packs tomorrow."*

A Chance Encounter With Andy Rhodes

"**H**OW ARE YOU FOLKS DOING?" The loud truck that had passed us as we walked over the empty highway bridge in the dark, had turned around, come back towards us and was now stopped in the middle of the road. The driver had hopped out, left the door open, and was calling out to Ras and I. We were both a little thrown off, nervous even, when the truck came back in our direction after already having gone past. Ras pushed me toward the shoulder of the road, interposing himself between me and the truck. Neither of us really knew what to expect. We were on a highway heading out of Safford, the largest of the trail towns. We had stayed a night in a motel there, picked up a resupply box, enjoyed some delicious food, and were now hitting the trail again. It was just past dusk. We had skirted the cotton fields for several miles as we first left Safford. Now we had this short highway shoulder walk before we got back onto the trail. We were looking for a large wash, when the truck and the voice interrupted our forward progress.

The man walked towards us in a friendly way and his voice became familiar to Ras and I as soon as he said "It's Andy Rhodes!" We had met Andy, who was on horseback and had three dogs with him, in a remote drive-up camp in the Pinaleños just a handful of days before. He had ridden through our camp while we readied ourselves one morning. The trail we had seen him on was rough and rugged. As we followed his horse's hoof prints up the steep, dusty trail, I thought of him and was impressed with how far he had ridden. We climbed and climbed, stopping to get water from a fresh flowing creek. Finally, we saw his golden retrievers come running towards us, ahead of Andy on his return trip down the trail, back to his camper in the campground where we had met him earlier that morning. He let us know a little bit about the trail ahead, and then we said goodbye as he rode off down the trail. He had made an impression on me then and I had written about him and his crew in my journal. He had told us that he lived by the "Thrifty" (how we thought it would be spelled) grocery store and to look him up when we were in Safford. When Ras and I saw the "Thriftee" (actual spelling), we thought of Andy but were caught up in our town tasks and never looked him up. I think it would have been a matter of asking a cashier at the grocery store about him, and we would have been sent in the right direction.

But now, a little on edge just outside of town in the darkening night, it was a relief and a pleasant surprise to have it be Andy who was calling out to Ras and I. We assured him we had been doing fine, caught him up on what we had seen and experienced since we had met him on the trail, and marveled in the synchronicity of it all. Andy was on his way home after teaching a taxidermy class at a place just up the highway. We passed it after we said goodbye to Andy and continued hiking along the shoulder of the highway, heading for the wash that would lead us out of Safford and back into the lonely wilderness.

* Day 18 3/21/17 Journal Entry*

18 miles yesterday! Wash outside of Thatcher/Safford. 7.5 miles to go to reach food and bathe, rejuvenating. Lots of Firsts on this route: climbing mountains while bush-whacking at night; descending boulder gullies at 1:30 a.m.; descending creek with rushing crossings in the dark; climbing and descending on steep snow fields; reaching 10,000 ft. in elevation; bush-whacking 1 mile along a desert mesa at night with prickly pear, barrel cactus, hidden rocks, possibilities of snakes. So technical, challenging, amazingly tough. The GET, son! *

Kathy Vaughan
March 26, 2017

Packing up camp & wondering where the trail will lead next. Morning in camp is pleasant; sipping coffee, organizing gear and food for the day and jotting down a few notes in my journal. Ras and I have settled into our trail routine and pack set-ups. It's all pretty simple, leaving room to focus on strength of mind, body and spirit.
#ZeroLimits. #RunStronger. #Team7Hills. #BeTrailReady. #TakeLessDoMore. #Getityoyo #PureNaturalEnergy

Ras Vaughan is with Kathy Vaughan.
March 26, 2017 · Instagram

GET YO-YO, DAY 21 - I LOVE MOVING THROUGH BEAUTIFUL AND CHALLENGING PLACES. Inhabiting such spots even only momentarily feels like an honor of which I am unworthy, as though at any moment someone will cry out, "There's the interloper! Sieze him!" And that sense of having slipped past the cosmic bouncer, as it were, makes each experience that much more valuable and helps me appreciate it that much more. What a Blessing to be a Hominid! Give Thanks for Life!

#GETyoyo #GETit #GrandEnchantmentTrail
#ZeroLimits #RunLonger #TakeLessDoMore #BeTrailReady #Team7hills #HShive

> **Ras Vaughan**
> April 18, 2017
>
> GET Yo-yo, Day 21 - Slot Canyon Walk Through on the Safford-Morenci Trail
> https://youtu.be/dYVd7tf_4SQ
>
> #GETyoyo #GETit #GrandEnchantmentTrail #TakeLessDoMore #ZeroLimits #RunLonger #BeTrailReady #Team7hills #HShive
>
> **GET Yo-yo, Day 21 - Slot Canyon Walk Through on the Safford-Morenci Trail**
> Ras and Kathy are attempting the first known yo-yo of the...
> YOUTUBE.COM

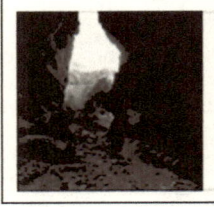

GET Yo-yo, Day 21 Video Transcript

Slot Canyon Walk Through On The Safford-Morenci Trail

Ras: *"Right now we are on the Old Safford-Morenci Trail, which used to be kind of a farm-to-market route for farmers in this area. And we're hiking up the Midnight Canyon wash and there's just a cool spot here where it narrows into this slot canyon. Realistically, to get a sense of it you don't need a lot of words from me."*

Kathy: *"Wow, look at that bolder lodged up near the top. This is the narrowest canyon we've been through so far."*

Ras: *"Man, what an amazing Blessing just to be able to move through beautiful places like this. There's another stopper stone up at the top of the canyon here."*

Kathy: *"Another mile back we saw a granary, an Anasazi cliff dwelling, as well."*

Ras: *"We're certainly not the first people to come through here, even this millennium. For a millennium or multiple millennia Human Beings have made use of these places where there's obvious consistent water."*

Kathy: *"It's a nice temperature in here."*

Ras: *"And these, as you can see, are some steps that were mortared in place, even with rebar. Presumably these are from the days when this was a pack *trail, to help horses and mules and the animals the farmers were using to transport their goods to the mines to sell. To get through here, it would be tricky footing for a quadruped, especially one burdened with a large load, without some sort of assistance."*

Ras Vaughan
April 18, 2017

GET YO-YO, DAY 22, #1 - Eagle Creek Beaver Jobsite
https://youtu.be/n168lsuPWYs

#GETyoyo #GETit #GrandEnchantmentTrail #TakeLessDoMore #ZeroLimits #RunLonger #BeTrailReady #Team7hills #HShive

GET Yo-yo, Day 22, #1 - Eagle Creek Beaver Jobsite

Ras and Kathy are attempting the first known yo-yo of the Grand Enchantment Trail. Along Eagle Creek, outside Morenci, AZ, they find some prime examples of b...

YOUTUBE.COM

GET Yo-yo, Day 22 Video Transcript

Eagle Creek Beaver Jobsite

Ras: "We are in Lower Eagle Creek outside Morenci and Safford, Arizona, and there is a lot of beaver activity in here, which is really cool; took down this big tree. It's impressive when you look at this and look at the size chips that this beaver's throwing. I mean, that's just crazy. Beavers are really

49

amazing creatures, and they really change their habitat and their environs to suit their purposes."

Kathy: "This is a big tree, and look, there's another one up there. There's a very active beaver right in this area of the creek, for sure.

Ras: "And then this one he felled and then, you can see, he bucked it up and he hauled off the top, took this big limb off here, limbed it all the way up, just like a logger. It's pretty interesting.

Kathy: "Or just like you do when you're out cutting firewood. It's exactly like that."

Ras: "Here's another tree that he felled."

Kathy: "And it's recent. This is all fresh, a fresh chew and fresh chips, for sure. Some of it's older beaver activity in here, so it's been happening for years."

Ras: "They're just these amazing creatures, and it's a blessing to get to see their work first hand."

> **Ras Vaughan**
> April 18, 2017 · Coupeville
>
> GET YO-YO, DAY 22, #2 - Another Fascinating Beaver Jobsite Along Eagle Creek
>
> https://youtu.be/1eWL5CVAZeo
>
> #GETyoyo #GETit #GrandEnchantmentTrail #TakeLessDoMore #ZeroLimits #RunLonger #BeTrailReady #Team7hills #HShive
>
> GET Yo-yo, Day 22, #2 - Another Fascinating Beaver Jobsite Along Eagle Creek
> YOUTUBE.COM

GET Yo-yo, Day 22 #2 Video Transcript

Another Fascinating Beaver Jobsite Along Eagle Creek

Ras: *"We've got another great example of a beaver job site here. Felled the tree, laid it out right toward the creek, and then at the end, you can see, he's peeled all the bark off and is cutting it to length, bucking it up. So, you can see, that's the size of a section, and then leaving another one of those sections, another pile of wood chips, out there again another pile of wood chips. So, he's already cut this tree into five or six pieces. Beaver at work."*

> **Ras Vaughan**
> March 27, 2017 · Instagram
>
> GET YO-YO, DAY 22 - THE IMPORTANCE OF FEELING SMALL AND INSIGNIFICANT is largely obscured in modern society. We are constantly told how important our every moment, thought, and desire is in order to sell us products which reinforce that notion. But as BadAss as Kathy may be, the juxtaposition of her beneath this giant cottonwood tree puts our Human ambitions and sense of self-import into perspective.
> What a Blessing to be a tiny, insignificant Hominid!
>
> #GETyoyo #GETit #GrandEnchantmentTrail #ZeroLimits #RunLonger #TakeLessDoMore #BeTrailReady #Team7hills #HShive

* Day 25 3/28/17 Journal Entry

Food cravings: candy, salad, fries, sandwich, drinks, ice cream, good pasta, mushrooms, sprouts and fresh onion. *

> **Ras Vaughan**
> April 18, 2017
>
> GET YO-YO, DAY 28 - Frigid Fords on Mineral Creek & Unwelcome Snow
> https://youtu.be/x_EigiqcIPY
>
> #GETyoyo #GETit #GrandEnchantmentTrail #TakeLessDoMore #ZeroLimits #RunLonger #BeTrailReady #Team7hills #HShive
>
> ### GET Yo-yo, Day 28 - Frigid Fords on Mineral Creek & Unwelcome Snow
> Ras and Kathy are attempting the first known yo-yo of the Grand Enchantment Trail. Heading east out of Alma, AZ, they pass through the historic mining distri...
> YOUTUBE.COM

GET Yo-yo, Day 28 Video Transcript

Frigid Fords on Mineral Creek & Unwelcome Snow

Ras: *"We were getting ready to get going this morning. We were climbing up out of Alma, New Mexico, yesterday, and a beautiful sunny day along Mineral Creek Road, which is like six miles of just fun fast road walking. We picked up a resupply at the Alma Store and had a great time talking to people there and getting some treats and catching up on some calories ...*

Kathy: *"Learning the history of Alma."*

Ras: *"As soon as we kit the Mineral Creek Trail it was shin deep fords. We had just picked up new shoes, which are now soaking wet. That's part of it, but it's not exactly how we were picturing things going. So, we were doing these creek fords last night and checking out all this cool old mining construction. These stacked stone buildings, the ruins of those, and that was all pretty cool and exciting. We found a nice little sandy spot just up from the creek, when our feet got painfully cold, to make our camp. Woke up this morning hoping to get going and it just got windier and colder as we were eating and getting ready to go. And now, as you can see, the weather is just deteriorating and getting worse and worse. So, there you go, it is snowing, so, for now, we are holing up in the tent and eating and organizing and getting ready to make our move for the day. But our shoes are already wet and we know we've got more creek fords ahead of us, so it really doesn't make sense to get into that any sooner than necessary. And just to give you another idea of what's been going on here that's interesting is, look at this sand everywhere. This super fine silt blew in through the night, throughout the night, came in through the mesh of our tent."*

Kathy: *"All over everything. It's in our cups."*

Ras: *"So it's a really interesting combination of challenges we're dealing with at the moment."*

Kathy: *"And the creeks fords are rushing water and it's cold water in this cold weather, so it's making our feet ice cold after five or six crossings."*

Ras: *"Pretty challenging. So, I've got my dirtbag down booties on which I made out of the sleeves off of an old down coat."*

Kathy: *"And I've got two pairs of wool socks, one of them coming way up my leg."*

Ras: *"We've both got our full puffy suits on and we're gonna eat a bunch of food and as soon as there's a break in the weather we will make our move."*

The Greatest Fail of Our Life

Ras Vaughan is with Kathy Vaughan at Mogollon Baldy.
April 4, 2017 · Instagram

GET YO-YO, DAY 29 - ASTERISK NUMBER ONE: We made the difficult decision to take the High Country Bypass and High Water Bypass routes around the Mogollon-Baldy trail and the West Fork Gila River.
Climbing up from Alma, NM, we had to ford Mineral Creek numerous times. It was swollen with snow melt and the water was frigid. We had to stop numerous times to make coffee and warm up our painfully cold feet, so much so that we burned through all our stove fuel, which we had been unable to resupply in Alma.
We then climbed out of Mineral Creek up to 9,000 feet, our shoes never fully drying. As we started to climb up the Crest Trail to top out at 10,400ish feet, it began snowing, and it increased as we climbed. With wet shoes and no stove fuel, we decided we needed to take the bypass routes in order not to jeopardize the entire project. So this will add an asterisk to our OKT, but it's what we had to do to salvage the overall yo-yo attempt while adhering to our feet-on-the-ground ethic.
What a Blessing to be testing our skills and limits in such beautiful and challenging environs! Give Thanks for Life!

#GETyoyo #GETit #GrandEnchantmentTrail
#ZeroLimits #RunLonger #TakeLessDoMore #BeTrailReady #Team7hills
#HShive

Day 29 4/2/17 Journal Entry

We borrowed a funky, heavy, and much appreciated stove from Jim, the outfitter with the mules at the Fish and Wildlife cabin at Willow Creek Campground. We had run out of fuel and he offered. We will leave it for him at Gila Hot Springs, where we will pick up a resupply and hope to buy fuel for our own stove while there. Ras saw a big flock of wild turkeys *

> **Ras Vaughan**
> April 18, 2017
>
> GET YO-YO, DAY 30 - Willow Creek, High Country & High Water Bypasses, & OKT Asterisks
>
> https://youtu.be/-4fyH2zd8KM
>
> #GETyoyo #GETit #GrandEnchantmentTrail #TakeLessDoMore #ZeroLimits #RunLonger #BeTrailReady #Team7hills #HShive
>
> GET Yo-yo, Day 30 - Willow Creek, High Country & High Water Bypasses, & OKT Asterisks
> YOUTUBE.COM

GET Yo-yo, Day 30 Video Transcript

Willow Creek, High Country & High-Water Bypasses, & OKT Asterisks

Ras: "Things are spinning out of control, getting away from us. We've hit some crazy weather, had a storm come through yesterday while we were trying to go up high onto the Mogollon Baldy route, which would have been up at 10,000 feet. And as we were starting to climb up it was snowing and starting to snow harder. And it just didn't make sense to be climbing and hoping th snow would stop. We're out of stove fuel and our feet were still wet from all of the fords on Mineral Creek. So, we decided to take the high-country bypass and ended up down here at Willow Creek. Met some good folks. This is Tyler Wallin and Jim Brooks who were kind enough to come over and check out our tent this morning and offered us a pot of hot water, which was an amazing blessing. And there's peanut butter and tortillas in store for us. They've just been generous and kind like you expect on the trail from country people but modern folks don't expect from one another. So, Jim, tell me your impression of the snow pack and the creek conditions right now."

Jim: "Well, we were here a couple weeks ago and it's down a lot from what it was, maybe half. This has been probably one of the better winters for snow in the last ten years, still maybe barely average. But this is kind of one of those storms you can never predict, but they show up and it's fast and furious and it's gone and in a couple of days it'll be in the 60's, so not bad, not bad. Weather should get better the whole time, but you might see another storm. Who knows."

Ras: "Oh, probably. I would expect so. So, we took the high-country bypass and we're gonna take the high-water bypass as well, which ads on a bunch of mileage. So that's gonna be asterisk number one on our Only Known Time. But it's just what we gotta do. So, we're still just enjoying the blessings of this adventure and having fun being in over our heads and dealing with making decisions and routing around what we have to and pushing through what we can."

Kathy Vaughan added 19 new photos from April 4, 2017 — with Ras Vaughan.

April 4, 2017

New Mexico is a beautiful place. Ras and I have seen so much and had such amazing moments of synchronicity. We've met cowboys and ranchers; seen javelinas, wild turkeys, elk, hawks and creek trout; found our way through damaged creek drainages and mountain ranges; I've face planted into a prickly pear cactus near midnight, causing Ras to pull spines from around my eye trailside; we've made a little fire to burn pinon sap and take in the fragrant scents of nature. Our progress on this route is slower than we hoped, but perfect, none the less. Giving thanks. #AltraRunning. #RunLonger. #PureNaturalEnergy. #Team7Hills. #Getityoyo. #GrandEnchantmentTrail. #BeTrailReady. #TakeLessDoMore. #ZeroLimits

* *Day 32 4/4/17   Journal Entry*

21 miles yesterday! Yay! Cruisy moving through pine country. After out last break, only 2ish miles from our goal, I took a hard fall into a prickly pear cactus with rock underneath. It had barely started to rain. I was wearing my cape. It affected my peripheral vision. The trail narrowed and got rocky. It was horrible. I screamed for Ras "Help me! Help me!" He didn't know what had happened. I'd been moving so well all day. He set up a triage center to begin pulling spines out of my face, from around my eye- left eye only, thankfully. He was so patient. They were all down my side, stuffed in my puffy pants and jacket. He helped me out of the pants and put his on me so I'd stay warm. He worked on all he could get out initially. I pulled some out of my hands. Luckily, I had brought tweezers. Then we prepared to hike towards a camp spot. The wind howled and we were on a narrow ridge. We had to hike at least a mile before we found the nice spot where we are now. There are still spines around my eye, tiny. My eye is swollen and black and blue. I also injured my knee and quad. I hope to be able to hike the 8ish miles into Gila Hot Springs without issue. I love Ras. He handled it all so well and he had to wear my reading glasses to pull spines out. *

Ras Vaughan is with Kathy Vaughan.
April 5, 2017

GET YO-YO, DAY 33 - A VERY BAD THING HAPPENS:
"HELP ME! PLEASE, HELP ME! PLEASE, HELP ME!" Kathy screamed over and over, her hands clutched to her face. We had been hiking our 20th mile of the day, it was nearing midnight, and it had just started to rain. We had just stopped to put on our rain capes and started hiking again when Kathy's steady footfalls were suddenly interrupted with a catch and a whump. Kathy had caught a toe on a rock, her arms and feet had hung up in her cape, and she had faceplanted on the side of the trail, and she began screaming in pain and fear as soon as she hit the ground. I ran up to her thinking, incorrectly, that one of her trekking poles had hit her in the face. But understanding dawned as she turned her bloody, spine-studded face up to me and the full horror of what had happened was revealed: she had landed in a prickly pear cactus.
Nothing makes you feel more worthless and powerless than having your favorite person in the world crying out to you for help in fear and pain as you stand there dumbfounded with no idea what to do. Eventually I snapped out of it, pulled her up out of the cactus, sat her down nearby, and pulled the spines nearest her left eye out with my fingers, Kathy still screaming for help the entire time. I don't know how long she cried out like that, but it felt like an eternity.
When I thought the immediate peril to her eye was past, I moved her over a few feet under a Juniper and out of the rain, dug the tweezers out of her pack, and began plucking the cactus spines from her lovely face, reassuring her the entire time that I was there to help her and that she was going to be

okay, even as she winced and cried out in pain with each clump of spines I pulled free.

When the pain got to be too much for her, I let her work on her own hand as I removed her rain cape and puffy pants, which were pincushioned with spines and had taken the brunt of it. I took off her waist pack, then removed some spines from her arm, hip, and leg. I covered the spines in Kathy's waist pack and puffy pants with duct tape and bundled up her cape and wrapped it with tape so the spines wouldn't migrate into other pieces of gear or clothing. Kathy began to get cold, mostly from shock I think, so I got my puffy pants out for her. I removed a few spines from her jacket, but it was otherwise okay. I worked on her face a little more, as we figured out what to do.

We were on a ridge, with no workable tent sites, so I got Kathy ready to hike until we could find a spot to set up for the night. Within a mile I found a suitable spot, set up our tent, and got Kathy out of her clothes and into the tent. Then, with the tweezers, Kathy's reading glasses, and my headlamp on high, I painstakingly removed all the spines I could find from my Beloved's face, arm, hand, hip, and leg. She had also landed on rocks, suffering bruises to her hip and knee, the latter of which causing her much pain during the short hike to our tent site.

About three hours from the time of her fall, Kathy was finally comfortable and calm enough to lay down to sleep. I settled into our shared sleeping bag next to her, thinking how much worse it could have been, and thankful that her eye had been spared. Seeming to read my mind, as we drifted into a traumatized sleep, Kathy said, "I guess it could have been a lot worse. It could have been a Cholla."

#OneBadAssLady
#GETyoyo #GETit #GrandEnchantmentTrail #TakeLessDoMore #ZeroLimits #RunLonger #BeTrailReady #Team7hills #HShive

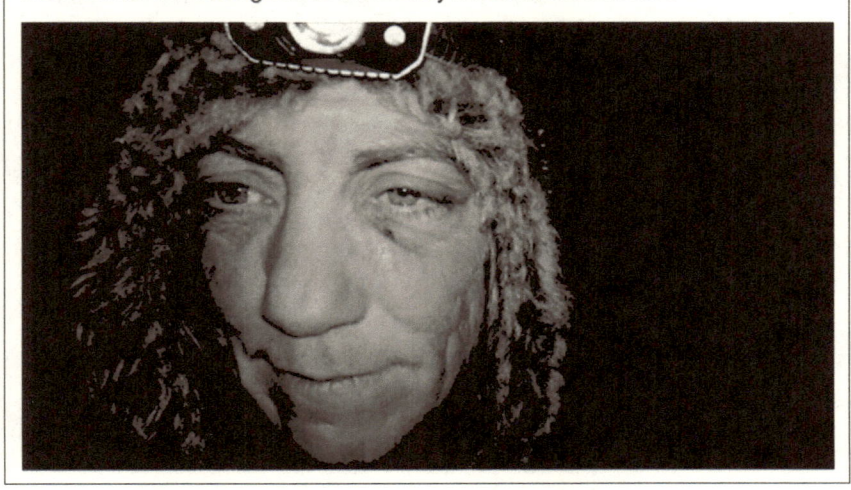

Ras Vaughan is with Kathy Vaughan at Doc Campbells Post.
April 5, 2017 · Instagram

GRAND ENCHANTMENT TRAIL YO-YO ATTEMPT, DAY 35 - PUSHING LIMITS IS WHAT TEAM ULTRAPEDESTRIAN IS ALL ABOUT, both our own limits and those of our gear. Shown here, Ras is taking the Gossamer Gear Mariposa 60 to its limits and beyond, with the assistance of the new Gossamer Gear Cuban Fiber Pack Liner. Facing a 189 mile section of the Grand Enchantment Trail without resupply, less gear means the ability to carry more food and do more backcountry mileage without having to make contact with civilization.
What a Blessing to be a Hominid!

#GETyoyo #GETit #GrandEnchantmentTrail #TakeLessDoMore #ZeroLimits #RunLonger #BeTrailReady #Team7hills #HShive

Kathy Vaughan
April 17, 2017

A harmless little cactus in all it's glory. The desert gives us blessings, both little & grand. I am well, healed & digging from reserves I did not know I possessed. The Grand Enchantment Trail is a blessing in my life and the land I'm passing through has blessed many before me. Give Thanks for Life! #Getityoyo. #AltraFromHeadToToe. #RunLonger. #HSStinger. #BeTrailReady. #TakeLessDoMore. #Team7Hills. #GrandEnchantmentTrail

> **Ras Vaughan**
> April 18, 2017
>
> GET YO-Yo, DAY 38 - Emergency Metallurgy, Stone Age Tools, & Backcountry Wedding Band Removal
>
> https://youtu.be/q_39wVL7ONI
>
> #GETyoyo #GETit #GrandEnchantmentTrail #TakeLessDoMore #ZeroLimits #RunLonger #BeTrailReady #Team7hills #HShive
>
> ### GET Yo-yo, Day 38 - Emergency Metallurgy, Stone Age Tools, & Backcountry Wedding Band Removal
> Ras and Kathy are attempting the first known yo-yo of the Grand Enchantment Trail. When Kathy's ring finger mysteriously swells, her wedding band becomes dan...
> YOUTUBE.COM

GET Yo-yo, Day 38 Video Transcript

Emergency Metallurgy, Stone Age Tools, & Backcountry Wedding Band Removal

Ras: "We just had to do some emergency metallurgy on Kathy's wedding band, because something happened to her finger and it got swoll up, that particular finger, it got really swollen and her wedding band was just tight on there. We don't know if she jammed it in her fall a few days ago and it's just now showing. Compared to that, though, very swollen. So, this is now what remains of her wedding band. And that is what remains of my beloved toenail clippers, which is one of my favorite tools in my MacGyver kit. Her wedding band is white gold so it's a relatively soft metal, so what we started off trying to do was to just use the toenail clippers and cut through it like a pair of wire dykes. And that was when we broke the handle off. So, then we had her wedging her had up like this with the ring sticking out ..."

Kathy: "I was pushing on the back of the ring to get it to stick out."

Ras: "... And we were getting the clippers on like that and then tapping them with a rock, so I eventually completely broke those as well. We had actually been able to cut about halfway through the ring at that point, but the toenail clippers were demolished, and we couldn't use them anymore. So, we had to apply Iron Age knowledge of metal, and how it gets more and more brittle when it's worked back and forth, with Stone Age tools, that literally being this stone and this stone. And she just carefully would place her finger like that, so the ring was pushed up in a loop and I would tap it until it was oblong. And then I would turn it ninety degrees and tap it down again until it was oblong, turn it back ... and we had it so that where it was partially cut through was the point where it was flexing. And it just got easier and easier to do, and then one time I was tapping through, tapped it flat and went to turn it and it was broken and I was able to just peal it off. So, a MacGyver moment as far as emergency wedding band removal, and another minor success on our Grand Enchantment Trail yo-yo."

* Day 39   4/11/17   Journal entry

More trail drama yesterday. My ring finger got swollen and Ras had to "cut" it off my finger – 20 years I wore the band. Also, saw a string of pack animals and 3 guys. The 1st cowboy was on edge, young, panicky, when he saw us. He asked us to wave & say hi to the horses. We did. The 3rd horse bucked & went off a bit. He dropped his lead. The final cowboy was rad – experienced, laid back, deep voice, big brimmed cowboy hat and a lot of facial fuzz. He whistled a tune as we made our way off trail to go around the string. Kinda cool. I don't know what they were up to. Thirdly, we saw a front leg of a deer or smaller elk, hung up on the top wire of fencing, fur on leg still, rest of body GONE – no trace. A bit further on the fence was down & the animal could have crossed there without losing its life. I cried thinking of its suffering and recalling the suffering deer I'd seen on the shoulder of the highway, in the snow one night, crossing over Steven's Pass, needing help. The look in its eyes. Last night, we got water from a "tire trough" on BLM ranch land. As Ras filtered the water, I looked all around, the moon & stars, the silhouettes of the mountains surrounding us. We were on two-track through somewhat flat and open prairie grassland. All of a sudden, a bright ball fell from the sky. I thought it was a falling star. But just before it disappeared, a red flashing light shone from the top of the yellowish gold ball. So bizarre.

This morning in camp, off in the distant grassy hills, I saw an animal other than a cow. It was paler in its coat color. Suddenly, it ran off & I could see it was an antelope. Then, while hiking, I saw movement out of the corner of my eye across a draw to my right. I stopped & looked in that direction. Faster than any animal I've ever seen run, was another antelope. I couldn't tell for a minute if it might be a large bird, like a hawk or other raptor. But it was indeed a prong horned antelope flying across the steeply sloped grassy draw. It was an impressive sight. Super-duper fast!!

My finger is still swollen. Not sure why. Jammed? Reaction to a sting or bite? So bizarre. Painful, but not throbbing or causing crying or whining.

We bathed and laundered out of Ojo Caliente today, a warm stream with good flow. We had to then hike a go-around of the Monticello Box. The road is public, but private owners say "No Access". It looked very scenic. Mile 502 Magdalena 85 miles from here – Bobtail Tank *

Ras Vaughan is with Kathy Vaughan in Continental Divide, New Mexico.
June 29, 2017

WILD PLACES DON'T SUGAR-COAT THE REALITIES OF LIFE.
Our modern society perpetuates the illusion of safety, security, predictability, and control. But the truth is that Life is short, fragile, and exceedingly valuable.

I am in no way as graceful or powerful as an elk. I don't move through challenging terrain as easily or efficiently or competently as Brother Elk does. Yet even a beast so impressively well-suited to the rugged high-altitude trials of life on the Continental Divide can fall prey to simple misadventure.

On the section of the Grand Enchantment Trail that uses 40-ish miles of the Continental Divide Trail, Kathy and I came upon this gruesome spectacle. As occasionally happens, an elk leaping this barbed wire fence failed to clear the top wire and it's leg got twisted up in the wires, snaring it. I imagine it bellowing in pain and fear, inadvertently attracting not help, but predators and scavengers. By the time we hiked by there was not a single trace of the bulk of the animal, just this disembodied leg suspended in the air to remind passersby of the fleeting nature of existence and the harsh realities of the natural world.

What a Blessing to be Alive!

#GETyoyo #GETit #GrandEnchantmentTrail #FeetOnTheGround #ZeroLimits #RunLonger #TakeLessDoMore #BeTrailReady #Team7hills #HShive

> **Ras Vaughan** is at New Mexico.
> April 19, 2017 · Instagram
>
> GET YO-YO, DAY 44 - FIRST RATTLESNAKE OF THE TRIP.
> This cute little guy came out to say hi, our first rattlesnake sighting after almost 580 miles!
> What a Blessing to be a Hominid!
>
> #GETyoyo #GETit #GrandEnchantmentTrail #TakeLessDoMore #ZeroLimits #RunLonger #BeTrailReady #Team7hills #HShive

* Day 44 4/16/17 Easter Sunday Journal Entry*

*Heading into Magdalena today – 28 miles. Feeling better. . . . . . Hungry, but we got this! We each have enough soakies and some chia seeds for the day. Filthy! It's beautiful here – cactus, steep slopes, birds singing. We saw a black widow spinning her web and a baby rattler, acting tough *

> **Kathy Vaughan** is with Ras Vaughan.
> April 18, 2017
>
> Hanging out in Magdalena today, resting our weary bodies; eating food including a delicious fresh salad; and washing clothing, our motel proprietor kindly allowing our use of her laundry room and giving us spaghetti squash for dinner last night. Our goal was no "zero" days, but we succumbed. It feels like the right decision as we ride the rhythm of this adventure. Give Thanks for Life!
> #ZeroLimits #BeTrailReady #Team7Hills #TakeLessDoMore #RunStronger #Nathan #GETityoyo. #PureNaturalEnergy. #AdventureTogether

* Day 46 4/18/17 Journal Entry

We began eating some cheese after hitting Alma on the trail. Hunger kicked in. I'm shocked here at the motel to see our weight loss. We had a spaghetti squash, quesadillas with whole pintos and fresh onion, donuts & coffee, root beer and Kickstarts. Ras had canned spinach and canned pineapple and popsicles.

We ate and rested.

The town is quite awesome. *

Kathy Vaughan
April 18, 2017

It's hard to be in New Mexico and not see, hear about or taste their red or green chili's. This string hangs outside our knotty pine room. Huge ponderosa and bushier pinon are in lovely forests up high, mixed with fir, spruce and aspen groves. Descending, prickly pear, cholla and small barrel shaped cactus join the mix. Juniper is up high and in the desert, changing in size. Alligator juniper trees in the higher elevations have character and are old and big. Grasses, agave and wildflowers are everywhere, the agave spears kinda showing off with their height and seed pods.
#GETityoyo #ZeroLimits #BeTrailReady #PureNaturalEnergy #Team7Hills. #GrandEnchantmentTrail #RunLonger

Ras Vaughan is with Kathy Vaughan in Magdalena, New Mexico.
April 19, 2017 · Instagram

GET YO-YO, DAY 47 - AS A RASTAMAN I CALL THIS PLACE A TRUEBRARY, but regardless of what One calls it, it's a crucial public resource. Small, middle of nowhere towns still rely on these centers of knowledge and communication in ways that larger communities may not. But itinerant populations such as thru-hikers still know their value.
Give Thanks for Truebraries and the Truebrarians who oversee them!
What a Blessing to be a modern Hominid!

#Truebrary
#GETyoyo #GETit #GrandEnchantmentTrail #TakeLessDoMore #ZeroLimits #RunLonger #BeTrailReady #Team7hills #HShive

Day 48 4/20/17 Journal Entry

San Lorenzo Canyon, Segment 32 - We had to reapply for our health care plan online at the library while we were in Magdalena. Once on the dirt road, ranchers and locals were passing, maybe five rigs. One rancher with his long flat-bed trailer pulled over. He gave a friendly "Howdy!", then warned us about a dog up the way. He said it has run out and crept under his truck to bite his lower leg. It was a Basset Hound. His driveway was just up to the left. He said he'd pull in it and wait for us to pass by before he drove in. He did. He killed his engine and waited. It was way cool and we thanked him for his kindness. He was leathery, wore a wedding band, maybe our age, cowboy hat and plaid shirt in blues. He'd been out getting firewood in cut poles, not yet bucked up. I really appreciated his kindness to us. Dogs can be gnarly and we'd had a dog act aggressively towards us in Magdalena. It's scary. A lot of people out here love hounds. 170 miles to the turn-around at Sandia! *

Ras Vaughan is with **Kathy Vaughan** at **New Mexico**.
April 20, 2017 · Instagram

GET YO-YO, DAY 48 - MOVING THROUGH BEAUTIFUL AND CHALLENGING PLACES IS SUCH A BLESSING. Ease of access can cheapen an experience by dint of not having invested of yourself sufficiently to make the payoff seem valuable. But a vantage point gained only by a brutally grinding climb, a secluded slot canyon cloistered by pour-offs and scrambling, or a wooded ridge cloaked in the thin air of high elevation are all made that much more precious by the investment required to experience them. So invest in yourself. Don't settle for the easily attained.

What a Blessing to be Alive! Give Thanks for Life!

#GETyoyo #GETit #GrandEnchantmentTrail #TakeLessDoMore #ZeroLimits #RunLonger #BeTrailReady #Team7hills #HShive

Ras Vaughan is with Kathy Vaughan in Polvadera, New Mexico.
April 21, 2017 · Instagram

GET YO-YO, DAY 49 - FORDING FAIL: TURNED BACK BY THE RIO GRANDE.

"Stubbornness trumps skill and training," I always say. But deep, fast-moving rivers drown even those as stubborn as I. When Kathy and I reached the Rio Grande this morning we hoped to be able to ford it, although we really didn't expect to be able to. Still, I stripped down and waded in looking for possibilities. I was quickly up to my waist with soft silt shifting beneath my feet and the fast, deep channel still 60 feet further in. It was an obvious no go. So we are now hiking out the High Water Bypass to access a bridge across the Rio Grande. It's the safe decision and the right decision and it's the way we expected it to play out. But there is a little part of me which is screaming in frustration at having been thwarted; at having had another's will imposed on me.
What a Blessing to be a Biped! Give Thanks for Life!

#GETyoyo #GETit #GrandEnchantmentTrail #TakeLessDoMore #ZeroLimits #RunLonger #BeTrailReady #Team7hills #HShive

Kathy Vaughan
April 21, 2017

The ford of the Rio Grande is a no go
Ras waded in to evaluate. It's too deep and fast. We will have to hike 6.5 miles to the bridge and then a bunch of other miles to get back to the trail. Safety first. Three huge geese were floating peacefully when we first arrived. It's nice to hear the wind rustling through the leaves and a rich fragrance is in the air from the spring buds on the trees.
#ZeroLimits #RunLonger. #GETityoyo #GrandEnchantmentTrail #BeTrailReady #PutrNaturalEnergy. #Team7Hills. #TakeLessDoMore. #AdventureTogether

Ras Vaughan is with Kathy Vaughan in Pueblito.
April 21, 2017 · Instagram

GET YO-YO, DAY 49, #2: BROTHERS & SISTERS, FRIENDS &FAMILY, PLEASE BE CAREFUL AND PLAY IT SAFE.
I don't know when we'll have a cell signal again, but even though we're traversing ridgelines at midnight, scrambling over pour-offs in slot canyons, and passing through the territories of cougar, bear, and wolves, the simple fact is that very few people die of misadventure in wild places. However, civilization, where you all are, is an extremely dangerous place where thousands of people meet their end everyday. So be careful out there and look out for one another!
Cooperation is the best survival strategy!

#GETyoyo #GETit #GrandEnchantmentTrail #TakeLessDoMore #ZeroLimits #RunLonger #BeTrailReady #Team7hills #HShive

> **Ras Vaughan** is with Kathy Vaughan at Black Mesa.
> April 24, 2017 · Instagram
>
> GET YO-YO, DAY 50 - SPEECHLESS.
> For realz, Universe? Astounding places like this exist and I'm only now finding out about them? So much to do! So much to see! So many reminders of how humble are our meager Human achievements!
> What a Blessing to be a tiny little Biped in such a big amazing World!
>
> #GETyoyo #GETit #GrandEnchantmentTrail #TakeLessDoMore #ZeroLimits #RunLonger #BeTrailReady #Team7hills #HShive

Ras Vaughan is with Kathy Vaughan at New Mexico.
April 23, 2017 · Instagram

GET YO-YO, DAY 51 - MANY PEOPLE DON'T REALISE THAT KATHY IS A PANCREATIC DISEASE SURVIVOR. Ten years ago she had 40% of her pancreas removed, as well as her spleen. This inhibits her ability to metabolize fats, limits her to smaller meal sizes, and makes her more susceptible to dehydration. Despite all this, she has repeatedly sought to test her mettle in the desert, where her medical history presents even more of a challenge. By pursuing unique achievement in the specific environs that present the greatest challenge to her, Kathy embodies the Zero Limits lifestyle like no one else. And that's only reason 374 why I love her and why she will forever be my OBAL.
It's a Blessing and an Honor to be a part of her life and adventures.
What a Blessing to be Alive!

#OneBadAssLady
#GETyoyo #GETit #GrandEnchantmentTrail #TakeLessDoMore #ZeroLimits #RunLonger #BeTrailReady #Team7hills #HShive

Kathy Vaughan is with Ras Vaughan.
April 24, 2017

112.8 miles to Albuquerque! We should be turning around and retracing our steps to Phoenix in less than a week. It feels amazing to have traveled this far by foot through so many different landscapes. My love and I are feeling at one with our surroundings. My mind is busy with so many trains of thought, wandering as I do, along the route. Our goal is 45 days to completion of the Grand Enchantment Trail yoyo. This will be a big push for us, but it's our A goal. Give Thanks For Life!
#ZeroLimits #BeTrailReady #RunLonger #Team7Hills #GETityoyo. #TakeLessDoMore #HShive.

* Day 52 4/24/17 Journal Entry

Yesterday, our last water source was at Ranch Headquarters, mile 650. We hiked 23 miles all together. The ranch house was quite beautiful, with an antique wooden door for the gate, fitted into the adobe wall, and a Virgin Mary tiled into an adobe wall in the front porch entry way. So nice of them to share water out here along this dusty, dirty road.

Ras is off now looking for a water source rated 3 (out of 4). I am having some solo time and I've gotten a lot done – soakies for both of us; cleaned and KT taped my right big toe; ate oatmeal with raisins and took my enzymes; enjoyed a yummy fauxcha (mocha made with an instant coffee packet and a hot chocolate packet mixed together); spiritual time with incense and prayer; lotioned up; braided my hair; put my pack together for the day; organized my garbage; and I will brush my teeth; Yay!

Kathy Vaughan is with Ras Vaughan in 📍 Phoenix, Arizona.
April 26, 2017

Back on the Pine Shadow trail after resting in the tent all day yesterday, the wind howling, rain & snow pellets hammering the tent and at 7,000 ft. In elevation. It feels good to be on the move again. The wind is still blowing, but the sun is shining & the dust has settled. Embracing all that comes our way, helps us appreciate the journey. Now, we keep climbing the well graded switchback trail to 10,000 ft where we get to take in all the views.
#ZeroLimits. #BeTrailReady. #RunLonger. #GETityoyo #PureNaturalEnergy. #TakeLessDoMore. #GrandEnchantmentTrail #Team7Hills

Ras Vaughan is with Kathy Vaughan at New Mexico.
April 26, 2017 · Instagram

GET YO-YO, DAY 54 - ALL DAY THE DAY BEFORE YESTERDAY I FELT SLUGGISH AND LIGHT-HEADED. At sundown, when we stopped to have dinner and transition into night-hiking mode, we found ourselves at the Pine Shadow trailhead. It was a wonderfully inviting spot, with tall Ponderosa Pines, bear proof trashcans, a Forest Service sh!tter, and a beautiful, flowing spring. It was essentially an oasis of infrastructure that proved too good to pass up. Considering my compromised state, we decided to make camp early, enjoy the accoutrements, catch up on some sleep, and get an early start the next day. Before turning in I invested about an hour attempting field fixes on blown out zippers that had been troubling us for days to escalating degrees. I managed some success, and Kathy and I cuddled into a taught, tight tent.

Except that the next day the weather turned to crap. We were awakened by our tent rattling and bucking under brutal wind gusts as huge rain drops pelted it with the force of a pressure washer. I braved the elements briefly to reinforce the tent and make runoff trenches around it and was thoroughly soaked in the process. (I even had to rig trekking poles as shears to create a high point over which to run a guyline for improved water shedding.) We ended up taking an unplanned zero day as it stormed, and awoke to a beautiful and sunny, if blustery, day, my field repairs finally failing, our zippers once again blown out.

Onward and Upwards! Forward ever, backwards never! What a Blessing to be a Biped! Give Thanks for Life!

#GETyoyo #GETit #GrandEnchantmentTrail #TakeLessDoMore #ZeroLimits #RunLonger #BeTrailReady #Team7hills #HShive

Day 54 4/26/17 Journal Entry

On-Trail Tips for Good Mileage Days

Be up & ready early

Eat breakfast & 2 cups coffee if possible

Keep pack weight down on town trips/resupply

Use tools staggered – wait to listen to mp3 player, caffeine later in day, etc.

Eat & nibble all day long

Sip water all day long

Be grateful

Be positive

Do lists, categories in head

Be helpful

Hike with purpose

One foot in front of the other

Make good layering decisions before putting on pack

Climb purposefully

Take focused breaks

Use treats – Tiger & Lip Balms, gum, salve, drink mix, mint/chamomile tea – For rough times

Listen to full book

The sun is setting behind me. I have hot coffee & hummus soup. We just tromped through a few miles of snow. Ras is off getting water 1/3 mile away. He always lets me rest & goes to get the water if it's off-trail. So kind. *

Kathy Vaughan is with Ras Vaughan.
April 26, 2017

I love and appreciate this guy so much. He is one of a kind. I'm glad he came into my neighborhood more than 20 years ago, looking for new Schwann's Frozen Food customers. I wanted him to come back, so I bought some frozen stir fry veggies from him. He came back and the rest is history. #GETityoyo. #AdventureTogether. #ZeroLimits. #BeTrailReady #Team7Hills. #RunLonger. #TakeLessDoMore #PureNaturalEnergy

Ras Vaughan is with Kathy Vaughan at Gila Wilderness.
April 27, 2017 · Instagram

GET YO-YO, DAY 55 - WE'RE ALL GONNA DIE! ... eventually. Our time is short and Life is so precious, so don't SPEND it, INVEST it! Live the Life you love and love the Life you live. Be the unique You that you were born to be. Do something crazy or creative or subtle or even sublime! Put something good and unique into the World to affect others, and leave our planet a better and more interesting place when you exit than when you arrived. What a Blessing to be a Alive! Give Thanks for Life!

#GETyoyo #GETit #GrandEnchantmentTrail #TakeLessDoMore #ZeroLimits #RunLonger #BeTrailReady #Team7hills #HShive

* Day 55 4/27/17 Journal Entry*

*We came down off the windy ridge trail we'd been on for hours, in the dark of the night, and met up with a dirt road. We hiked by towers and power centers and what not; so much noise with the wind and the circuits! Eerie! We hiked the dirt road uphill and met up with a car camp, complete with 3-sided shelters, garbage cans and shitters. Now, we are huddled under a shelter, sheltered from the relentless wind. Towns are visible far below. We saw the glow of Albuquerque last night. It's real. It's happening. We will arrive. *

Kathy Vaughan is with Ras Vaughan.
April 26, 2017

A fresh dusting of snow in The Manzanos.
#GETityoyo. #GrandEnchanrmentTrail. #AdventureTogether

Day 56 4/229/17 Journal Entry

*Ras woke up jacked to get to Ray's One Stop, so we left at 7:40 a.m., our earliest start yet. We had made it there in time for lunch and to get more miles in for the day. We had hiked so hungry, our stomachs grumbling, empty pits. My blood sugar, or glucose tolerance, or whatever, bottoming out over and over again. *

Ras Vaughan is with Kathy Vaughan in Tajique, New Mexico.
April 28, 2017 · Instagram

GET YO-YO, DAY 56 - I LOVE STORES IN LITTLE MIDDLE OF NOWHERE TOWNS! Ray's One Stop in Tajique, NM, was our first taste of civilization in a number of days and had most of what we needed. Moreover, they let us use their microwave to zap up some food as well as hang out in front. Then, when warning us of the forecast for snow tonight, offered us a place to stay for the night. We had to demure, but what a a Blessing to be treated with such kindness by an absolute stranger!
What a Blessing to be a Hominid! Give Thanks for Life!

#GETyoyo #GETit #GrandEnchantmentTrail #TakeLessDoMore #ZeroLimits #RunLonger #BeTrailReady #Team7hills #HShive

* Day 57 4/30/17 Journal Entry

Sunshine Market, Hwy 377 walk, 14 miles, Tajique to Sunshine Market, then 2 ½ miles to FS land to camp. Wow! What an adventure! Culvert Camp worked well until take off time this a.m. We awoke to leave. Ras wanted to do a video. I didn't know that. I instead was having to pee, having strong thirst and knowing we were low on water. I filled my water bottle 2x with snow from the top of the culvert, being careful not to get the dirty snow from the shoulder where the plowed snow had been piled up. I had been eating Fritos- heavy salt and MSG. I think that is where the extreme thirst had come from. It awoke me in the night. Our tent zippers are malfunctioning. I had to go out his side each time, putting on my shoes, while he moved out of the way; coming back inside with culvert mud to knock off my shoes first. He would comment each time, "Wow, again?" So, in the pre-dawn hours, I held it miserably. I exclaimed internally as the opening to the culvert brightened and I could tell dawn was coming. Ras would wake up and I could finally pee and drink. By morning, I came to tears over the stress. We didn't know where we would get water again. The sun was out, but the wind was blowing terribly. This was a shitty way to begin a shitty highway walk after a day and a half in a culvert underneath a highway, waiting out a snow storm. *

Ras Vaughan
May 1, 2017

GET YO-YO, DAY 59 -COUGARS, CULVERT CAMP, AND COMMUNITY MARKETS; A RECAP OF RECENT REALITIES.

Day 55 - Just as we reached Upper4th Of July Spring at around 10:30pm it started to rain in earnest. We put our capes on as we were pelted with large drops. I filled one water bladder from the spring-fed trough. As I turned back toward Kathy to fetch the other bladder my headlamp beam swept the trail downhill of us (where we would be continuing on) and it stopped on the dumbfounded face of a young cougar. He stared back at me agape for a moment before he turned a black-tipped tail to me, then scrambled up the rock face beside the trail and peered down at us. The rain had obscured our noise and scent, so we surprized him by being at his water trough. I was unnerving to walk below those rocks, but we saw no more of the big cat.

Day 56 - After hiking a quick seven morning miles we hit Ray's One Stop in Tejique for a few quick calories. We were warned of an approaching snowstorm and offered a place to stay, but we decided to push on. Eight miles later, after numerous brief showers, as we were hiking along the shoulder of NM377, it began to rain in earnest. We stepped into a culvert running under the highway to have a snack and wait out the squall. We then watched the rain turn to snow, and the snow begin to accumulate. We were dry and our gear was dry, so it made no sense to go out into the storm. I jerry-rigged a tent set, and we spent the night in what we came to call Culvert Camp.

Day 57 - We awoke to about a foot of snow on the ground, and more falling, and realized we weren't leaving Culvert Camp anytime soon. I found the local public radio station on the FM band of my mp3 player and heard the forecast of snow tapering off overnight and mostly sunny with highs in the 50s the next day. A full day and second night in Culvert Camp was dry and protected from the wind and snow, but relatively boring. I did some gear repairs and made a stove from two energy drink cans, as well as building two small dikes and a water channel to protect our tent site in case of massive melt during the night.

Day 58 - Bright sunshine awakened us before our alarm and we knew it was time to get heck out of Culvert Camp, as grateful as we were for it. We climbed out of the culvert, up onto the shoulder of the highway, and straight into a 20+ mph headwind which we battled for the next 16 miles. We enjoyed brief respites at the Ten Points General Store a little north of Escabosa, and the Morning Star Market in Ponderosa Pine. From there we pushed on to the Turkey Trot Trailhead and camped in the parking lot, since it was snow free and gravel, which had drained well. A young bowhunter named Andrew, out after turkey, told us it had snowed 14 inches there. A little later a nice guy named Josh (a fellow thruhiker we lived nearby) invited us by for coffee and breakfast the next morning. So many people have been so generous and kind to us.

Day 59 - We awakened to find Andrew had snuck by early in the morning and left us two apples, two bananas, and a giant avocado. We headed toward Tijeras under bright sun.

What a Blessing to be a Hominid! Give Thanks for Life!

#GETyoyo #GETit #GrandEnchantmentTrail #TakeLessDoMore #ZeroLimits #RunLonger #BeTrailReady #Team7hills #HShive

Kathy Vaughan is with Ras Vaughan.
May 2, 2017

There is nothing like making friends with fellow thru hikers on the trail! We met Max way back by Picket Post trail head in the Superstitions. By Magdalena, he and Steady had connected on the trail and were hiking together. Yesterday we saw them coming towards us on the trail, as they had changed things up a bit. Steady is a Triple Crowner and very accomplished thru hiker. She said this is the toughest route she's done.

Today, Ras & I set out to teach the lower Sandia aerial tram terminal, our turn around point, trail mile 770. We have hiked 42 additional miles, to uphold our "feet on the ground ethic". This means we have hiked all of the off trail miles to reach resupply towns, no hitchhiking around the 28 mile road stretch where no public camping is allowed, and includes a 189 mile stretch without hitting a town/ resupplying. True to the thru. Bring on the yo!!! #ZeroLimits #RunLonger #BeTrailReady. #TakeLessDoMore. #HShive. #GETityoyo. #GrandEnchantmentTrail.

Albuquerque: Bounce Point Achieved

ON DAY 60, RAS AND I REACHED the Sandia Aerial Tram on the edge of Albuquerque, the official turn around point for our Grand Enchantment Trail Yo-yo. We were ecstatic to have reached this crucial point in our journey. Just before hitting the Tram parking area, Ras and I sat down in the shade of a tree, trying to absorb the feelings we were both having about finally approaching the turn-around, and legitimately needing a shade stop from the hustle we had been putting in during our morning hike. Suddenly, a young man with a running vest and water bottles up front came around the bend. He stopped short at seeing us and with a nervous voice asked if we were Ras and Kathy. He was about 16 years old and appeared to know exactly who we were. We both answered in a friendly way that we were indeed Ras and Kathy of Team UltraPedestrian. He said he had gotten out of school in just enough time to get to the La Luz trail, which we had been descending since the previous night, to say hi and congratulate us on having completed the first leg of our Yo-yo. He had been following our SPOT Tracker and knew approximately where we would be. As his hands quivered, Ras asked if he would like to get in a selfie shot with us. It was such a fun moment. He was clearly inspired by us and the effort we had been putting forth for 60 days now. He was not on social media,, and we really didn't know how he knew of us. He was starting out on a trail run and seemed anxious to get moving down the trail and not hold us up. We assured him that it was great meeting him and he in no way had delayed us. He could have joined us if he wanted to, as we finished off our trek to the Tram lot, but after a friendly goodbye, he ran off down the trail.

Ras and I got up from our rest, now filled with encouragement and the reminder that we had folks keeping an eye on our progress. We hugged and got a photo in front of a sign that said, "Slow Pedestrians", which we found quite fitting. We had expected to reach Albuquerque long before this day. The GET was giving us quite a dose of challenge, mixed in with unending beauty and solitude. We were anxious to get turned around and start our trek back to Phoenix; but for now, food.

The Sandia Aerial Tram had a nice, but expensive, restaurant in the Visitor's Center, and we lucked out by having the coolest, most understanding server ever. This young gal was totally hip, and catered to us in a most respectful way, Ras and I both knowing we looked and smelled like hiker

> **Ras Vaughan** is with Kathy Vaughan in Sandia Foothills.
> May 3, 2017 · Instagram
>
> GET YO-YO, DAY 60 - CONSTANT ASS-WHOOPINGS BY THE GRAND ENCHANTMENT TRAIL.
> As we complete the first of our two Yos, it's tempting to say that the Grand Enchantment Trail has kicked our butts at every opportunity. And it's certainly true that it's an incredibly difficult route, with its unmaintained trails, bushwhacking, cross-country portions, copious burned and flood damaged sections, intense cattle impact, wash walking, navigational challenges, and scant on-trail resupply options. And the weather hasn't done us any favors, either. High water, rain, constants scouring winds, and snowstorms have had us wading through creeks for days on end, hunkered in our tent for 36 hour stretches, chapped and wind-burned, and postholing through snow anywhere from ankle to thigh deep.
> But the fact of the matter is that we chose to attempt our yo-yo according to a strict feet-on-the-ground ethic, not accepting rides or hitchhiking into resupply towns, covering every mile of the GET as well as our off-route resupply mileage under our own power and on our own two feet. This ethic doesn't make for the fastest or prettiest going, but it makes for the best Style, in an Alpinist sense. And since this is an Only Known Time attempt, we don't have to beat anyone else's time. We simply have to complete the route. And adhering to our FOTG ethic is far more important to us than shaving days or even weeks off our time, even when it means waiting out a snowstorm in a culvert for two days.
> We are Team UltraPedestrian, and moving through Beautiful and Challenging places is not only what we love to do, but what we must do to be true to ourselves, be the best that we can be, and, hopefully, to add a little good and positivity to the world.
> What a Blessing to be a Biped!
> Give Thanks for Life!

trash. She even said we were fortunate to have gotten her as our server. She helped us choose out menu items that would fit our hiker budget and laughed with us as we made self-deprecating jokes in reference to how long we had been on the trail. She was fascinated with our journey and goal to hike back to Phoenix. We gave her an UltraPedestrian sticker and went on our way.

Ras and I loved the architecture and the surrounding mountainous view of Albuquerque. We had not intended to spend any time there, but without much convincing, we decided to hike the 7 miles into the area of the city

#GETyoyo #GETit #GrandEnchantmentTrail #FeetOnTheGround #TakeLessDoMore
#ZeroLimits #RunLonger #BeTrailReady #Team7hills #HShive

where we could shop at Trader Joe's & Albertsons, get a strong coffee and cold drinks, interact with other human beings for a day, and wash our clothes and ourselves. It was a great decision, and even though it took time away from our actual trail trek, it helped recharge us for what lay ahead.

We ended up getting our motel room comped as a woman with little yippie dogs caused a great amount of disturbance in the hallways, making it very difficult to get to the launderette and lobby area. We let a couple of incidents pass before Ras finally called the front desk to complain. The motel environment was a little sketchy. As we hiked away from it in the morning after our stay, a young guy called out to us, asking if either of us had

> **Ras Vaughan** is with Kathy Vaughan at Sandia Peak Tramway.
> May 3, 2017 · Instagram
>
> It was super kind of the Sandia Peak Tramway to install this custom sign welcoming us!
>
> #GETyoyo #GETit #GrandEnchantmentTrail #FeetOnTheGround #TakeLessDoMore
> #ZeroLimits #RunLonger #BeTrailReady #Team7hills #HShive

a cigarette. We answered that we did not, and continued hiking along the shoulder of the service road that paralleled I-40. He walked at a brisk, squirrely seeming pace.

The young man had been at a car, back at the motel parking lot, and my sense was that something questionable was taking place at that car. He seemed to be trying to get away from the area, as quickly as possible. I was very aware of his presence as he walked near Ras and I, both of us making our way towards the main arterial and freeway entrance ramp. Ras needed some epoxy to repair his trekking pole, so we were heading to Lowe's. I didn't know if Ras had his eye on this young guy still or not, but he kept talking to me

> **Kathy Vaughan**
> May 3, 2017 · Albuquerque, NM
>
> A hungry hiker meal- Portabella panini. So delicious! One yo down!!! Giving thanks for our safe passage.
> #ZeroLimits. #RunLonger #TakeLessDoMore. #GETityoyo. #PureNaturalEnergy. #Team7Hills

about something and didn't seem to be paying attention. I was very distracted, my 6th sense telling me to remain alert.

We walked into the busy parking lot, and I lost sight of the other pedestrian. I assumed he had walked off in another direction as we approached the busy arterial. But instead, as I waited just outside the front door with our backpacks while Ras went inside in search of the epoxy, he approached me as if we already knew each other. Instead of feeling as if I should be uneasy with this character, I got the sense that he needed a listening ear, a mother figure of sorts. And with my trail hardened appearance and tattered looking backpack, I caught the eye of this young man. He said something bad was going down, and he has been on a path to get away from trouble. He didn't want to be any part of it. I have no idea how serious the situation was back at the car in the near empty motel parking lot, but there wasn't anything I could do about it. What I could do, was for a few minutes, I could listen to this young guy express some fears and vulnerability. I could reassure him that staying away from trouble was a good idea. I could show warmth and empathy towards him for a few minutes. I could show some humanity towards a young man who needed it. Coming off the trail and right into the city, the juxtaposition is overwhelming. I like that I emanated a vibe of warmth, of love, and of the healing powers of the wilderness; that I was able to carry that with me off the trail and into Albuquerque.

Ras and I continued our walk back through Albuquerque, back towards the Sandia Aerial Tram where we could begin our return Yo. We stopped in Trader Joe's again to stock up on some food for the trail. We didn't have a resupply box to pick up in Albuquerque, but the variety and price of groceries at Trader Joe's was better than a box. We shopped around and had small cups of sample coffee. We chose out fresh foods, something to have for lunch, trail mixes for our packs and cold drinks to take with us for the rest of our hike through the city. We finished our shopping, and I felt as though I might pass out. We tried to sit at some tables out front of the store, and we became the subject of interest for several parties of shoppers. One lady was impressed with how fit we looked. Another wanted to know the specifics of our trek. I became overwhelmed and spotted a square of shade in front of a dumpster in the corner of the parking lot. I told Ras I had to get to that shade. I got there, pulled out my sleeping pad, and began to cool down. The queasiness persisted. I focused on taking in some water, relaxing and trying to create that balance between wanting some of the benefits of civilization, yet longing to be alone on the trail again, with just Ras.

Baseball games were being played by youth leagues in different neighborhoods as we continued along. The roar of cheering would erupt as exciting plays were made. We walked into the parking area of one of these baseball diamonds. A couple of dads were gathered around a pickup truck. A rattle snake was curled up in the spare tire compartment, and they were trying to get it out safely. I wondered how often this happens in the desert.

Ras and I both enjoyed looking at the adobe houses with brightly painted gates and trim, and rustic ladders leaned up against their sides, as if to help with access to an upper level like in ancient Pueblo dwellings. A mix of cactus plants of all varieties, pine and juniper trees, and early spring flowers grew in the yards. Paths of mixed shades of terra-cotta colored rocks completed the

The Greatest Fail of Our Life

> **Ras Vaughan** is in Sandia Foothills.
> May 4, 2017 · Instagram
>
> GET YO-YO, DAY 61 - YO NUMBER TWO HAS OFFICIALLY BEGUN!
> After one night in Albuquerque enjoying some necessary infrastructure, including much needed laundry and showers, Kathy and I are rejuvenated and motivated and back on the trail. The people of Albuquerque were amazingly friendly, and we are already making plans to return and explore more in the future. Everywhere we went folks did us extra little favors, and we were again offered a place to stay for the night. However, it would have required a ride in a vehicle and would have violated our Feet On The Ground ethic, so we had to decline, but the offer of kindness was itself a Blessing. (To show the degree to which we are attempting to honor the FOTG ideal, I even decided to forego the use of the elevator in the motel and took the stairs up and down to the laundry room.)
> We got just the right dose of civilization, enough to enjoy and appreciate it without taking it for granted, and we are headed back into the mountains and back into the Real World.
> It begins. This is it. Now it gets really real. This is uncharted territory, and this is where we love to be. We are way outside our original time goals, so we have devised updated goals. Our AZT YO-yo took 93 days. So matching that would be a pie-in-the-sky A goal. Fewer than 100 days is our B goal. And goal C, our baseline goal, is simply to complete the first known Yo-yo of the Grand Enchantment Trail. The only thing we're racing at this point is Summer.
> What a Blessing to be Alive! Give Thanks for Life!

yards, and most homes had inviting outdoor living areas. From the La Luz Trail that descends into the heights above Albuquerque, it was possible to see homes with pools or jacuzzies on upper decks, that reached up towards the open desert sky. The lights of the city glimmered in the dark night, thus the namesake for the trail toward which Ras and I were heading.

Ras and I made it back to the La Luz Trail and silently and non-ceremoniously began our trek back towards Phoenix. Our packs were bulging with the extra food we had picked up in Albuquerque. We hiked less than a mile before we found the perfect rock to have our dinner picnic. The sun had set and the night air felt good. I recollected the experiences I had in the city. I felt disconnected from the reality that Ras and I were hiking west now. It all felt very surreal. And then out of the darkness, a figure appeared on the trail. I saw big, curly hair underneath a large brimmed hat. The person did not have a headlamp but had a guitar or hand drum slung across his body. The trail ahead would become very rocky, steep and technical. The going would be rough without a light, and with no moonlight casting any glow to help either. I wondered what the story was here.

#GETyoyo #GETit #GrandEnchantmentTrail #FeetOnTheGround #TakeLessDoMore
#ZeroLimits #RunLonger #BeTrailReady #Team7hills #HShive

Ras and I finished our dinner and then hiked along again in silence. I had assumed the person without the light who had passed us earlier, was going to be sleeping alongside the trail. I kept a lookout but did not see anyone. The figure's whereabouts were now a curiosity to me. Suddenly, ahead in the trail, was a person in a sleeping bag. This figure in the dark was different, wearing a tight-fitting Mountain Hardware hiking cap and sound asleep nestled inside a sleeping bag. I could see the backpack set off to one side of the sleeping hiker. A single trekking pole lay by his side. This was not the curly headed solo wanderer from earlier. I made the assumption that this was a GET thru-hiker getting a final night's sleep on the trail. He would reach the eastern terminus of the trail first thing in the morning.

The Final Yo

> **Ras Vaughan**
> May 6, 2017
>
> GET YO-YO, DAY 61 - BOUNCE DAY! THE FINAL YO BEGINS!
> After a near-0 day in Albuquerque to do laundry and shower, they once again hit the trail, now on the return trip to Phoenix. Way behind schedule based on their original goals, they are now racing the onset of summer, hoping to complete their project before the debilitating heat of June hits.
>
> #GETyoyo #GETit #GrandEnchantmentTrail #FeetOnTheGround #TakeLessDoMore
> #ZeroLimits #RunLonger #BeTrailReady #Team7hills #HShive
>
> **GET Yo-yo, Day 61 - Bounce Day! The Final Yo Begins!**
> Ras and Kathy are attempting the first known yo-yo of the Grand Enchantment Trail. After a near-0 day in Albuquerque to do laundry and shower, they once agai...
> YOUTUBE.COM

GET Yo-yo, Day 61 Video Transcript

Bounce Day! The Final Yo Begins!

Ras: "Team UltraPedestrian beginning, officially, the second Yo of our Grand Enchantment Trail Yo-yo attempt. Yesterday we completed Yo #1, somewhere around 2:00 in the afternoon, I can't remember exactly, and we then hiked on into Albuquerque. We'd never gotten a chance to really see Albuquerque at all or explore it, and we wanted to do that. Plus, we were sorely in need of the use of a little bit of infrastructure. We had not had a chance to do laundry or take a proper shower or bath since Magdalena, which was a heck of a while ago. So, it was definitely much needed and a bit overdo. So, we got to catch up on some chores and self-care and get a good amount of rest and enjoy a little bit of Albu-quirky. And now we're back doing what we love to do, getting on the trail. We enjoyed that taste of civilization, and a little over twenty-four hours is just about what's right for us on that. And we're both definitely ready to get back into some wild places, and that is what we're doing. So, Yo #2 of the Grand Enchantment Trail Yo-yo."

Ras Vaughan shared Kathy Vaughan's post.
May 6, 2017

GET YO-YO, DAY 63 - EVERY TIME YOU HEAR A THRUHIKER BELCH A TRAIL ANGEL EARNS THEIR WINGS.

#GETyoyo #GETit #GrandEnchantmentTrail #FeetOnTheGround #TakeLessDoMore
#ZeroLimits #RunLonger #BeTrailReady #Team7hills #HShive

Kathy Vaughan added 4 new photos.
May 6, 2017

What a guy! Adam Delu, a fellow @Altra Ambassador from Albuquerque, met Ras and I on the trail yesterday. He was so fun to hike and visit with, as we worked our way up to the Sandia Crest. When we got to the parking lot, he proceeded to unveil the most gourmet picnic ever!!! Strawberries, pineapple, cucumber, carrots, apples, oranges, Dolmas, hummus with pine nuts & on & on. He loaded up our packs with more and then joined us for more miles on the Crest. It was a perfect send off on our 2nd Yo and a blessing to connect with another trail and Altra enthusiast. I feel like I made a new friend. Give Thanks for Life!

> **Ras Vaughan**
> May 7, 2017 · Instagram
>
> GET YO-YO, DAY 64 - WE'RE SUPPOSED TO BE MASHING MILES, but I get easily distracted when the locals come out to cheer us on. Looking At Lizards and Staring Awestruck At The Beauty And Variety Of Creation might be clumsy priorities to put into words, but they are both definitely way up there on our list of things To Did.
> What a Blessing to be Alive! Give Thanks for Life!
>
> #GETyoyo #GETit #GrandEnchantmentTrail #FeetOnTheGround #TakeLessDoMore
> #ZeroLimits #RunLonger #BeTrailReady #Team7hills #HShive

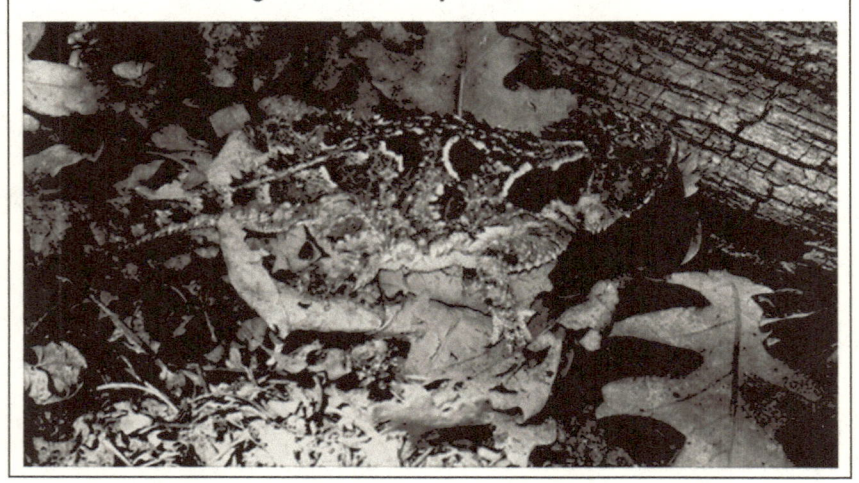

Kathy Vaughan
May 10, 2017

"Don't tread on me! I am the color of the earth and the world; therefore walk carefully, that you do not tread on me.". Look carefully to see both of the horned toads. I visited with the brighter one on the right, before even seeing the one on the left.
#GETityoyo. #TheManzanitas

Ras Vaughan is with Kathy Vaughan at Ten Points General Store.
May 9, 2017 · Instagram

GET YO-YO, DAY 65 - CULVERT CAMP WASN'T AS INVITING WITHOUT A FOOT AND A HALF OF SNOW ON THE GROUND. We cruised on past the spot where we sat out the big storm nine days previous, pausing only briefly to tempt fate with this selfie. We have now completed the 18 mile highway shoulder walk in each direction, and it feels great to have that over with. Mentally, that was the crux of the yo-yo. But we still have 700 miles to go, Summer is roaring in like a lion, and I'm sure NM and AZ still have plenty of tricks up their sleeves.
Forward Ever! Onward and Upwards!
What a Blessing to be Hominid! Give Thanks for Life!

#GETyoyo #GETit #GrandEnchantmentTrail #FeetOnTheGround #TakeLessDoMore
#ZeroLimits #RunLonger #BeTrailReady #Team7hills #HShive

Day 67 5/10/17 Journal Entry

Crest Trail camp, mud and burn zone. It snowed crazy hard, thunder and wind, along the Crest Trail. 13 miles. We pushed to the drive-up camp in the pines, with a Forest service outhouse, where we dried out, warmed up and ate dinner with a black widow. Her web contained the remains of the male which she had eaten. *

Ras Vaughan is with Kathy Vaughan at Sand Canyon.
May 11, 2017 · Instagram

GET YO-YO, DAY 67 - WAITING OUT A SUDDEN SNOW SQUALL, my head tucked into my rain cape. Pellet snow pummelled us as we hunkered down. We sat out some of the worst of it, but still spent most of the day hiking through snow, wind, and rain. Wild turkeys, Aberts Squirrels, deer, and rabbits were out and about, leaving the hieroglyphs of their tracks in the snow for us to decipher.
What a Blessing to be Biped! Give Thanks for Life!

#GETyoyo #GETit #GrandEnchantmentTrail #FeetOnTheGround #TakeLessDoMore
#ZeroLimits #RunLonger #BeTrailReady #Team7hills #HShive

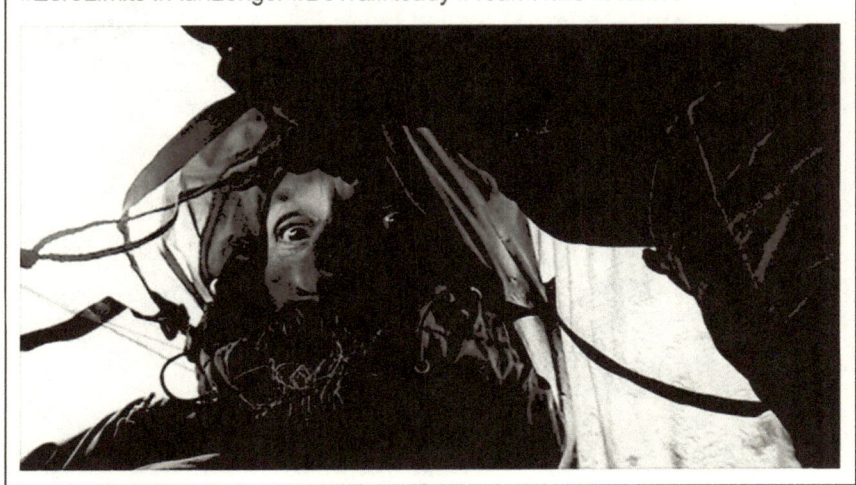

Kathy Vaughan
May 11, 2017

Yesterday's lunch break view as I huddled inside my rain cape in the Manzano Mountain Wilderness.
#GETityoyo. #GrandEnchantmentTrail #ZeroLimits. #RunLonger. #TakeLessDoMore. #BeTrailReady

> Ras Vaughan is at Sand Canyon.
> May 12, 2017 · Instagram
>
> GET YO-YO, DAY 68 - SCOPING OUT THESE COOL ROCKS I SUDDENLY FOUND TWO FACES STARING BACK AT ME. No, it wasn't my over-stimulated brain's pattern matching center finding faces that weren't there. Rather, it was a herd of Big Horn Mountain Sheep whose heads slowly popped up into view as we watched; first two, then another then six in total, although I suspect there were more concealed in the shade and not curious enough about us to interrupt their repose.
> What a Blessing to be Hominid! Give Thanks for Life!
>
> #GETyoyo #GETit #GrandEnchantmentTrail #FeetOnTheGround #TakeLessDoMore
> #ZeroLimits #RunLonger #BeTrailReady #Team7hills #HShive

* Day 68 5/11/17 Journal Entry

Awoke to sunshine and warmer temps. We will begin with road walking on dirt, then some 4-wheel drive track and wash walking. Got to get over 20 miles today! Ras will filter water here and we will be a-okay in that area. The wind gently blows and birds sing nearby. *

> Ras Vaughan is with Kathy Vaughan at New Mexico.
> May 13, 2017 · Instagram
>
> GET YO-YO, DAY 70 - WATER IS A SPECIAL BLESSING IN ARID AREAS. As with the AZT, many of the developed water sources along the Grand Enchantment Trail were established with commercial ruminants in mind. But if there's a Hominid interloper at their water source, they fall back and wait their turn.
> What a Blessing to be Biped! Give Thanks for Life!
>
> #GETyoyo #GETit #GrandEnchantmentTrail #FeetOnTheGround #TakeLessDoMore
> #ZeroLimits #RunLonger #BeTrailReady #Team7hills #HShive

* Day 70 5/13/17 Journal Entry

The wind was so strong on our 16-mile hike this morning, a headwind. The sun was blazing hot. We simply had to hike the dirt road, into it. We had to get to Lemitar to pick up our resupply box at the post office before it closed. We found some protection from the wind behind a big water tank and Ras called the post office. The kind man said he'd meet us with our boxes at 2:00 at the post office. He would come back after hours. So kind. He seemed interested in us and what our route would be from Lemitar. Then we went to the truck stop. *

Lemitar, Lovingkindness, and Leaning on Inner Strength

BACK AT THE SMALL TRUCKSTOP in Lemitar for the second time, we walked in a bit more confidently, finding the same table tucked back in the corner, and plugging our electronics and battery charger into the available outlet. We ordered cold drinks and fried foods and enjoyed just sitting. We looked into taking showers there and it turned out it was actually simple. We hadn't really thought of it on our way east. Ras paid the cashier at the grocery area of the truck stop and took the first shower to check things out. He had tons of time left afterwards, and after checking in with the cashier, I was allowed to go in and shower before the room got cleaned up in between the two of us. Thus, we were not charged a second fee for my shower time. It's nice to get a special deal like this, as our thru-hiking budget was pretty tight. I loved getting freshened up and washing away all of the trail grime. I walked out of that room feeling like a new person.

Someone in the small café must have noticed all of this, because the waitress walked over to our table shortly after having delivered our meals, to tell us that another customer had picked up our tab. I'm not sure exactly what it was about us that had prompted someone to want to pay our bill for us, but it was very kind and we definitely appreciated it.

After making a couple of purchases over in the mini mart section of the truck stop, we stepped outside to be on our way. An older white Suburban was parked alongside a curb, not necessarily in a proper parking spot, but not really in the way of other vehicles either. This same rig had been parked here when we were on our eastbound hike. I couldn't have not recognized it this second time through. It was jammed full of stuff and at first glance, looked like someone on a road trip. Upon closer examination, it looked like someone had all of their belongings in it and possibly lived within it. It would be easy enough to do in the desert climate. The days were heating up as our hike was leading us deeper into the spring weather here in New Mexico. I could see living in this desert climate myself, just out on the land. The owner of the vehicle soon appeared and had taken an interest in Ras and I. We were making a couple of last minute adjustments to our packs, at a picnic table that was near the curb where he was parked. He could tell we were on our feet by the size of our packs and the look of us, and soon started asking questions about our travels. We were polite, but still had our slight creeper alert on. We said goodbye and were on our way.

> **Ras Vaughan** is with Kathy Vaughan at Roadrunner Travel Center.
> May 13, 2017 · Instagram
>
> GET YO-YO, DAY 70, #2 - GOBSMACKED, WILLIAM SHATNERED, DUMBFOUNDED, WHATEVER YOU WANNA CALL IT I'M AT A LOSS FOR WORDS. The last 36 hours have been a mind-bending blend of striving, frailty, achievement, failure, and the humility born of receiving unwarranted kindness.
> Beginning Friday morning Kathy and I were attempting to complete a 43 mile push by 11:30AM Saturday in order to pick up two boxes of food and gear from the Lemitar, NM, Post Office during their limited weekend hours. After 27 miles the math was turning against us. We laid down to nap for an hour or two in a small cut at 5:30AM Saturday, mentally making back up plans for missing our parcel pick up.
> We woke up and began beating against a brutal headwind, our hearts despairing as we struggled to pound out our final 16 miles. At 11:30 I got a cell signal and was able to call the Lemitar Post Master just as the Post Office was closing. He generously agreed to meet us at 2:00PM with our packages, sacrificing hours of his afternoon to help two thru-hikers who were complete strangers to him.
> Then, in the cafe in the Phillips 66 truck stop, as we were organising our food into our packs, a waitress came over and pointed out an older couple who were leaving and told us they had paid our bill for us.
> It is humbling and inspiring to be the recipient of such kindnesses, and it makes me proud to be a Human Being.
> With all of the negativity and conflict and division portrayed in the media, these experiences remind me that there is a Kind American Heart, and that it is a very real thing, even if it doesn't make headlines.
> What a Blessing to be Hominid! Give Thanks for Life!

It was now turning to dusk and the day felt cooler. We had to walk under the highway overpass, alongside the curb past the Great Pyrenees' ranch that we had walked by earlier on our hike, and across a bridge over the Rio Grande before we started our hike along the Bosque. We planned on hiking for a couple of hours, before stopping at one of the established campgrounds with cement picnic tables, along the double-track route that paralleled a canal. We had seen white cranes, ducks, and other birds in the waterways heading east.

The Greatest Fail of Our Life

But now in the dark, it was quiet and peaceful as we strolled along, our bellies full from the Lemitar truck stop.

Just before reaching the double-track along the canal, we had crossed the bridge and were walking in the dark along the shoulder of a back road. We heard a truck coming along the road, loud and fast, voices of teens spilling out the open windows. I didn't like the energy from it, so we dipped back into the trees along the shoulder when the truck got close enough to pass. It stopped short up the road, and then came back our direction. Now we heard the voices of teen girls. They had picked up some girls when they stopped, and now it seemed like the potential for showing off had just grown. We again hid as they passed by in the fast truck, knowing that the reflections from our backpacks and other gear were possibly giving us away, despite our attempts to lay low. They sped off out of ear shot and soon, we were strolling peacefully through the empty park that would take us to the double-track.

#GETyoyo #GETit #GrandEnchantmentTrail #FeetOnTheGround #TakeLessDoMore
#ZeroLimits #RunLonger #BeTrailReady #Team7hills #HShive

We finally reached an empty campground and set up our tent. It was nice to sit at a proper picnic table and have a late-night snack before tucking into our sleeping bags. The following day would begin with an exposed hike through a long wash. Then, we would hike through the very scenic San Lorenzo Canyon, and into its narrows where we would fill water from the spring. Next, we would have dirt road mileage that would get us back to the

111

town of Magdalena. From there, we would have a two-night stay in our favorite motel, The Western, and 586 remaining trail miles to the completion of the GET Yo-yo attempt.

When we woke up the next morning, the heat of the climate along the river floor of the Rio Grande was felt by us immediately. It was Mother's Day. I was flooded with mixed emotions, as I sat at the cement table. I felt like taking my time getting ready that morning and having a big breakfast with a couple of cups of coffee. Ras had not mentioned anything about Mother's Day and didn't seem to remember. I hadn't gotten a message from Angela. But I reflected on all that it meant to me to be a mother to my cherished Angela, and the fading reminiscences of a Mother's Day when she was just 11 months old. Tears welled up in my eyes as I remembered that was the day her birth father had passed away and I had gotten news of it as I waited for him to arrive at my parent's home for a BBQ salmon dinner. It was late in the afternoon and I had an anxious and sinking feeling in my stomach, thinking he wasn't going to make it at this point. We had been living separately since before she was born. He was just coming for the day. We were holding up the dinner for him. The wife of his boss from his job as a carpenter had called to tell me. I cried "No, No, No!" I could never eat barbequed salmon again.

The strength I gained from enduring that type of shock and pain in my 20s, being left alone to raise a precious 11-month-old daughter who was just beginning to walk, was helping me through this insanely difficult hike. I was tapping into my deepest sense of courage and endurance, to push on each day and cover miles. I was going back to my inner hominid, to all that had made me who I was. I was using training that I had done specifically for the hike, as well as actual life experience, to assist me on this journey. I was feeling weak, with weight loss and hunger; it was simply too challenging to pack enough of the right calories to sustain the energy I was burning. I felt nausea sometimes, and unquenchable thirst at others. I was hot during the day, and chilled easily at night. I had a painful and bleeding hemorrhoid that caused me concern and discomfort. I spat blood when I brushed my teeth. The more I brushed, the more blood I spat, surprising myself with the amount of blood that would come out with the frothy toothpaste. In camp, this made for a messy toothbrushing scene.

On the other hand, my feet were holding up well and the muscles in my legs and core were at an all-time level of fitness. I had never looked so trim and sinewy. I probably looked too thin, and without a scale, I didn't know what I weighed or how much weight I had lost since I set foot on the trail near Phoenix, nearly several months ago. I know my clothes felt looser and I could feel my hip bones protruding. I just had to make it through the final 600 miles or so. I was so close to the end of this push.

Kathy Vaughan
May 16, 2017 · Magdalena, NM

Gossamer Gear rocks!!! They have super cool ultralight gear for backpacking/fast packing. They brought Ras & I on as ambassadors before we left for our #GETyoyo and the gear we got from them has been awesome- trekking poles, the Deuce of Spades (uh, for digging cat holes) cuben fiber gear bags with zippers, our 3/4 length sleeping pads and NOW THIS!! The silver sun umbrella on my pack is making the hot desert stretches manageable. It creates shade on the move and is very light to hold. I can position it however needed to block the intense sun and it deflects the hot rays. I am in love with this sunbrella!!!
#GossamerGear. #TakeLessDoMore. #GrandEnchantmentTrail. #GETityoyo

Wash Walking

SAND AT TIMES FEELS FIRM UNDERFOOT, making for swift hiking, and then at others, soft, slowing the pace as each footstep squishes into it. Wash walking can be a time when good progress is made, or a time when steady and slow forward movement happens with little thought to navigation. Washes are scenic, and at times technical to move through while hiking. In the Southwest, hiking through washes is going to happen. They are a constant throughout the terrain of the desert landscape and they do make for easy navigation. They sometimes lead to a creek. They can also lead to dirt roads. They take hikers through deep cuts in various layers of rock and sand, or through shallow depressions in the desert ground. On some of the stretches of trail, Ras and I spent seven miles or more at a time hiking through a wash. Sometimes they are hot and exposed with no chance for shade, like Putnam Wash until it reaches the spring, or they can provide shade from trees like cottonwood or juniper.

Some of the washes that Ras and I hiked through were rocky. Sometimes there were large boulders to climb around or scramble over, small rolling rocks to find the best path over, or sometimes huge rocky walls that had to be navigated around outside of the wash itself. Ras and I took a lot of breaks in washes, because we could find shade or a nice flat place to sit. We camped in washes as well, under the trees, or up against the wash wall. We only did this on nights without a cloud in the sky, the stars bright and shimmering above with a clear forecast ahead.

Our favorite wash in New Mexico led to Ojo Caliente, the warm spring that we hiked along instead of the route that once led through Monticello Box. We hiked through it late at night, and when we got to where Ojo Caliente came off the hillside and met up with the wash's end, we set up our camp. I looked for the depiction of a cartoonish calf face, which I had seen on our way east. There it was again, just where I had remembered seeing it. The calf's eyes were two very black but smooth rocks, spaced just the right distance apart. The calf had a cute look on its face as two other rocks, triangular shaped with tips, made the ears. I was happy that I had been able to remember just where this calf was in the rocky wall of the wash. Tree roots grew into the wash wall as well, exposed to the air as a bit more of the wall crumbles away slowly over time.

The Magdalena Post Office lady had told us about soldiers marching through the washes in the heat during the Mexican War. She said that the buttons from their heavy wool coats were sometimes found on the wash floor. I looked day and night for these buttons in all of the washes in the Magdalena area, as I hiked along. I never found any, but it got my imagination going and gave me something to look for as we moved through the washes.

Ras Vaughan is at San Lorenzo Canyon.
May 16, 2017 · Instagram

GET YO-YO, DAY 72 - FOR THOSE WHO MAY NOT GROCK THE SUPER-ADVENTURE-DORK-INESS OF WHAT WE'RE UP TO IN ALL ITS GLORY, our Yo-yo projects are based on a philosophical theory: the idea that the character of the trail, and ones experience of it, varies noticeably based on direction of travel. Completing a trail once in each direction in a single push may seem to some like splitting hairs, or like a parlor trick designed to manufacture a new FKT where one already exists. But to the UltraPedestrian mindset, a yo-yo is the best approach to experience a trail as completely as possible. That's our goal, and we think it's a worthy one; a pilgrimage a modern Hero's Quest, if youwill. And if not everyone gets it, that's okay, too.
What a Blessing to be Modern Biped! Give Thanks for Life!

#GETyoyo #GETit #GrandEnchantmentTrail #FeetOnTheGround #TakeLessDoMore
#ZeroLimits #RunLonger #BeTrailReady #Team7hills #HShive

The Mysterious Monticello Rock

THE HEAT WAS ALMOST UNBEARABLE. Ras and I had been hiking through a series of cross-country connections. We were on high, steep hillsides that we had to descend to a wash or ravine below, and then immediately regain the elevation we had lost by climbing up the next hillside. As we began to down climb one of these such hills, it became quite rocky with sharp-edged, sandstone colored rocks. As we were not on a clearly defined trail, Ras led the way, finding the best line to switchback down this somewhat dangerous slope. I could see the lovely canyon below and was anxious to find shade along the steep rock walls. I could see some trees and shrubs that would also help create some shade possibilities. I wondered if there might be water somewhere up the canyon. I remembered passing through here on our way east and had not seen any then. We had a little bit of water with us, but we were needing to reach our next source soon. We were on a section of trail that was bypassing a very scenic and special area called Monticello Box. Private landowners were not allowing hikers to pass through the box where the water flowed freely and could be a great source for thirsty travelers. Far below I could see a lush ranch with bright green fields and tall cottonwoods. This stood out in stark contrast to the dry, rocky lands surrounding it. Feeling hot and thirsty, I felt envious of this inviting scene below. Our trek would not take us through that countryside where a cool creek flowed and irrigated the land around it. Ras and I were instead being led down, down towards Kelly Canyon and a hope of water, but at the very least shade in its hold.

As we continued our tedious descent towards our break spot, Ras stopped suddenly. Something had caught his eye. A very unusual rock was lying there. The rock underfoot was flat and sharp-edged, sandstone colored and easily broke off in slabs. But this rock that had beckoned Ras' attention, was instead smooth and dark. It clearly was not natural to this environment. It had been carried here. Ras picked it up to examine it. It was heavy in my hands, as I took it from him to look at myself. It definitely seemed like an archaic tool. It had been smoothed out by something, we could see. Was it a from a distant river and had been carried here by a traveler many years ago, used as a tool necessary to their existence? Was it just a strange coincidence that an unusual rock was here, alongside our route, but was actually natural to this environment? The rock was elongated, about two feet long. It was pointed on either end, one end duller than the other. It fit so easily into our hands as we held it. Ras and I both sensed it had been used by humans before. It fit so well into our hands, it was hard to believe that we were the first humans to have ever held it in such a way. It looked like it could have been used to crush grains or roll out flat breads. It was far too heavy for us to carry with us, and we were so intrigued by it, we both forgot to take a picture. Ras laid it back down in the spot from which he had picked it up. We quietly went on our way, our heads spinning with the untold story of the curious rock.

About a week earlier, while staying two nights in our favorite trail town along the route, Magdalena, we had seen a flyer posted about a talk at the library that would be held on the evening of our second night there. The talk looked interesting to both Ras and I. It was entitled "New Mexico before Columbus". Ras, in particular, had done some studying about early hominids and we decided that this would be a relaxing and educational way to spend an evening. We had already been to the Magdalena library on our way eastbound on the trail. The librarian had been helpful towards us getting our health insurance information updated and renewed while on route. Outside the library were covered picnic tables with electrical outlets and a quiet, park-like setting. For thru-hikers, it was very inviting.

It felt awkward at first to be in an enclosed room with other people. All of the chairs were full and the room felt hot and stuffy. I had been very thirsty during our stay in Magdalena and kept drinking water, almost a half-bottle full at a time, struggling to quench an undying thirst. I was drinking fruit juices and sodas during this stay as well. I hadn't brought any water to the library, figuring drinks aren't usually allowed inside. I saw others with small plastic bottles of water and wondered if they had been handed out when the talk first began. I looked around to see if there was a table anywhere with bottles of water available. I couldn't stop thinking about water, or a cold drink of any kind. It was distracting. I had felt queasy while in the motel room, and although there were little tasks I had hoped to accomplish while in Magdalena, I was unable to do much at all. I lay on the bed, feeling nauseous and low energy and hoping it would pass. We almost decided against going to the library talk, but in the end I'm glad we went.

Once back to our sweet little motel room decorated in knotty pine interior, with a southwest flair, we readied ourselves to go to the motel owner's quarters for dinner. Dami had left a note on our door to come by when we got back. Her son, Dominic, was visiting her and he wanted to make us a vegan dinner. We had met him earlier in the afternoon. Ras gave him his Gossamer Gear pack that he had been using, as he had just picked up a new pack to test

Kathy Vaughan
May 17, 2017 · Magdalena, NM

Ras & I are in Magdalena, NM again. We really like this little town, the Western Motel, the friendly postal worker whose husband is a travel writer and the sweet little cafe with green salads and yummy sandwiches. We had to hang out to receive packages from Altra and a new tent, zippers all blown out on our Six Moon Designs tent. With high winds, scorpions, black widows, rattlers and the longest centipedes ever, messed up zippers is not an option. We will be back on the trail again first thing tomorrow morning, hitting our 190 mile stretch in remote territory with no resupply. It's getting real. We are working hard, losing weight, weathering all kinds of weather and still have nearly 600 miles left. I am drawn forward by the changing seasons- Aspen leafing out in the higher elevations, wildflowers blooming, creeks still flowing, a strong focus on a goal I've worked towards for months now, and pets & family awaiting our return. No pain, no gain they say. I know this truth from a lifetime of taking on what is before me, handling life's ups & downs the best I know how. Give Thanks For Life!
#ZeroLimits. #RunLonger. #Team7Hills #BeTrailReady. #PureNaturalEnergy #GETityoyo. #GossamerGear

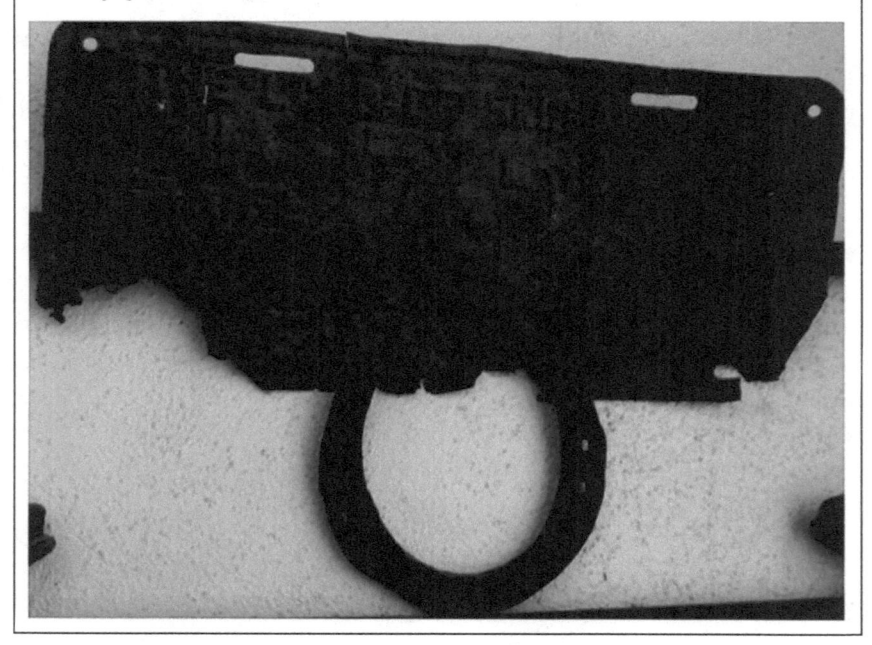

out on the trail from Gossamer Gear. We knew Dominic was going to be hiking with his son up to Mt. Whitney later in the season, and that one or the other of them might appreciate the pack. It turned out to be such a welcome gift for Dominic. He wanted to visit with us some more and help get some fresh foods into us. He had experimented around with a vegan diet several years prior and enjoys cooking.

Dami and Dominic showed us all around the historic adobe house that once served as a birthing hospital for the small community. The building was one of the oldest in Magdalena and had so much character. We gathered around the table afterwards and enjoyed guacamole; beans; pico de gallo; a huge salad with nutritional yeast and Bragg's Liquid Aminos (both favorite condiments we had not had in days); fresh carrot sticks; coffee and blackberry cobbler. It was wonderful.

I enjoyed visiting with Dami and Dominic and hearing about his efforts at earning his degree in physical therapy and his more than 20 years of experience as a karate instructor. Dami is Puerto Rican and I really enjoyed her kind, motherly energy with Ras and I. She was generous and giving from the moment we met her, bringing us a box with spaghetti squash, oatmeal, raisins, bananas, and dishes to use in the room when we first arrived. She later brought us some mashed potatoes and salad from her Easter dinner and offered to pick us up anything we needed when she drove to Wal Mart the next day. I will never forget her generosity and warmth.

At the time, I did not know the significance of the thirst and nausea, the talk at the library about early man and the tools they used, and how the special connection with Dami and Dominic would continue beyond the trail.

> **Ras Vaughan**
> May 18, 2017 · Instagram
>
> GET YO-YO, DAY 75 - MOTION IS THE GOAL. MOVEMENT. PROGRESS. To quote Jack London's legendary antagonist Wolf Larson, "I believe that life is a mess. It is like yeast, a ferment, a thing that moves and may move for a minute, an hour, a year, or a hundred years, but that in the end will cease to move. The big eat the little that they may continue to move, the strong eat the weak that they may retain their strength. The lucky eat the most and move the longest."
> What a Blessing to be Hominid! Give Thanks for Life!
>
> #GETyoyo #GETit #GrandEnchantmentTrail #FeetOnTheGround #TakeLessDoMore
> #ZeroLimits #RunLonger #BeTrailReady #Team7hills #HShive

GET Yo-yo, Day 81 Video Transcript

Ojo Caliente: The Miracle Of Water Pouring Out Of The Desert Soil

Ras: "I just wanted to show you something that I think is absolutely amazing. This is Ojo Caliente. See the frogs just jump in? And this is, as the name implies, a warm spring which is just a little bit from the mouth of the Monticello Box Canyon. And this is just something that amazes me. This just pops up right here. We've been hiking along a wash for miles. So, there's a wash miles uphill of this which is essentially a giant natural filter. And it collects all of that water and it moves underground and pops up right here. You can actually see, down in here, dust on the bottom being disturbed by the water percolating up out of the ground. And it's just astounding to be way out, miles and miles into these arid mountains, this high-country desert, and to come across a spot where water is just pouring out of the ground. And I'm moving downstream of the main little spring bowl here to show you ... there's a garter snake that just swum into the shadows over there ... but this is the flow. I've got to speak up so you'll be able to hear me over it. But this is the flow out of that little bowl back there; that much water. Gallons and gallons of water. That's gotta be 100 gallons per minute. Incredible flow. If you had a well you dug giving off this sort of flow you would be stoked. But this is just one of the amazing things that you see on the Grand Enchantment Trail. And that's part of why it's so important to get out into the natural world, and get out miles away from where other people are, and see the astounding things that our world has to offer. That's really an important part of our philosophy, of the UltraPedestrian philosophy, the UltraPedestrian ethos, and our Modern Hominid philosophy, is being in the world, being immersed in it, and being in a state of wonder at how incredible it is. With our modern society, and our amazing vehicles, and processed foods that show up on our tables, and all those other things, our scientific immersion I think gives us an illusion and understanding of the world which just isn't factual. And I can look it up, I can look up all of the mechanics behind what makes this spring pop up here, but that doesn't displace the sense of wonder of hiking for days and days and days through the desert and then suddenly finding water popping up out of the ground. And it's like seventy-five degrees, too. It's a warm spring, that's why it's named Ojo Caliente. It's just an astounding thing. And the life in here! There's all sorts of frogs that you saw leap into the water when I first came over, there's a garter snake swimming through there, there's all sorts of water striders and little water beetles and everything else. But especially in an arid place like a desert, water is so absolutely essential to many forms of life, especially animal life, this is an amazing place to see it. I'm sure that with a game camera in the night you could see some even more interesting visitors. I looked around for tracks, but it's kind of rocky, sandy, it doesn't hold tracks well, and there is a lot of cattle and stock activity in here, which obliterates just everything. One of the amazing blessings of our planet: Ojo Caliente, this incredible flow of water just popping up out of the ground in the middle of a high mountain desert."

Elk

WE SAT CROSS LEGGED ON THE HIGH MESA TOP, our own mesa for two, we called it. It was quiet and peaceful. Large pine trees stood spaced out nicely and we had camped under one we found particularly sheltering. The soft needles made for a comfy bed under our tent. There was a sense of quiet solitude; no other humans anywhere near us and no chance of anyone sauntering by. It was wonderful and perfect. Mornings in camp are my favorite times on the trail. I love drinking my coffee and scoping out the surroundings. Ras and I make camp in the dark each night. When we awake, we are seeing our environment with the new light of day and a refreshed perspective. Off in the distance, I felt a presence and saw a young elk, and then another. Soon a small herd appeared. These were the first elk that Ras and I had seen on the trail. We were often seeing the scattered droppings of the large animals. This herd appeared to be local, using the earthen tank nearby as their water source.

On our hike west after having turned around in Albuquerque, we experienced another chance at seeing elk, and not just their droppings. Ras and I were descending from the Continental Divide Trail. We had been following it for nearly three days now, hiking in elevations ranging from 8,000 to 9,000 feet. To come down off of this high divide, we followed a burn, green grasses and wildflowers now beginning to brighten up the dark landscape. Young aspen trees were returning to the area and were loaded with tent caterpillars. These cocoons they were making were hanging from the branches of the thick masses of these trees, everywhere we looked. The cocoons were loaded with the squirming caterpillars. It was an infestation and it looked unearthly.

As we continued to descend, we entered areas where huge pines still stood, unaffected by the fire. These areas of forest were shaded, dark, lush and inviting. And not only to Ras and I. We saw a very large critter in the middle of the trail up ahead and soon realized it was a very healthy-looking elk. The herd we had seen on our mesa for two were smaller in stature and were feeding in a different zone. This elk had access to a swift running creek that Ras and I would soon be following, Diamond Creek, and they were browsing on the lush grass and regrowth from the fire having swept through here some time ago.

However, this elk was not alone. Ras and I stood there silently, he taking pictures of the elk we both had spotted, and I hoping to not disturb the moment. Then, from some sunken bowl in the forest floor, a humongous set of antlers rose up slowly, cautiously, beastly. I could not believe the size of this guy. Several other large elk rose up from the hidden and cool napping spot.

Ras Vaughan
May 30, 2017 · Instagram · 🌐 ▼

GET YO-YO, DAY 84 - YET ANOTHER MACGYVER MOMENT ON THE GRAND ENCHANTMENT TRAIL. The nose piece to Kathy's sunglasses fell off and was lost, allowing me the opportunity to improvise a fix. I had super glue in my ever-present MacGyver kit, and realized the extra ear pieces from my mp3 player ear buds could be repurposed as a comfortable replacement nose piece.
What a Blessing to be Modern Hominid! Give Thanks for Life!

#MacGyverMoment #GETyoyo #GETit #GrandEnchantmentTrail #FeetOnTheGround #TakeLessDoMore
#ZeroLimits #RunLonger #BeTrailReady #Team7hills #HShive

The animals took off into the pine forest. I had felt small and insignificant in their presence. The racks on the heads of these creatures were unbelievably heavy looking. They made it appear effortless to carry these large sets of antlers, the giant racks somehow seeming proportional atop the head of such an enormous and handsome animal.

Further along the trail in another area, we found a skull still bearing a full rack of antlers. It was leaned up between two trees in a spot that has likely served as a camp, a time or two. Hiking along late at night, the glow of our headlamps caught the surprising sight of the huge set of antlers. It felt very smooth to the touch and had not taken any damage from rodents, or otherwise. It was very heavy. We took some pictures of it and then let it remain as we had found it.

In the very high country of New Mexico, elk, wild turkey, and squirrels, are about the only wildlife Ras and I encountered. There were many more elk walking where we walked, than would ever let themselves be known. For that, Ras and I held much respect. We hiked through these areas of solitude with the knowledge that we were being observed. To pass through with very little impact, was always our goal.

Diamond Creek Valley, which forks off at the confluence with Burnt Canyon from which we had just descended, is just about the most beautiful place I have ever hiked. After having forded the creek running through Burnt Canyon over and over again, pushing through overgrown brush, cautiously scrambling along rocky trail, Ras and I were entering a wide and lush valley. Wild Iris were growing in little clumps here and there. Diamond Creek babbled in spots and flowed gracefully in others. Tall, large-girthed pine trees stood guardian over the valley. I could have spent days and days here. The trail was easy to follow singletrack through grassy terrain. The valley widened and narrowed as we made our way through it. Sometimes rocky canyon walls rose up and other times another valley or canyon would feed into the main one through which we hiked. We stopped to lay down in the grass, rest and have a snack. Everywhere I looked, all around, were enchanting scenes. No one was in sight. There was very little chance of anyone entering this valley as Ras and I hiked through it.

To have a place like this to ourselves, almost every day on this trail to have these landscapes to ourselves, is very ethereal. Each day is spent quiet and looking inside, letting thoughts come and go, or grabbing ahold to explore more deeply. Some stretches of time are spent listening to music, or a book. But there are endless hours of only the sounds that nature provides – water flowing, birds singing, the wind blowing, the sounds of insect wings or buzzing, the refreshing sound of rainfall or the creaking of trees as they sway in the wind.

Kathy Vaughan
May 29, 2017

I enjoyed my first soak in a natural hot springs, starlit sky and all. Afterwards, Ras and I enjoyed a fire and conversation in the cave above with 2 Italian guys who heated up a can of cannelloni beans over the fire for us. We made it through our 189 mile unsupplied stretch with strength & guts. I feel strong & fit & ready to finish off our final 400 mile stretch. We saw a dark wolf, 2 elk with massive antlers, many little horned toads, a silver fox, cool lizards, blue herons, swarms of swallows, black widows, wild iris, cactus in bloom, wonderful cliffs and cliff dwellings and so much more. I love New Mexico and it's endless mountain ranges, washes and pristine canyons. I feel incredibly blessed to be on the #GrandEnchantmentTrail. #ZeroLimits #RunLonger #Team7Hills #BeTrailReady #PureNaturalEnergy #GETityoyo #TakeLessDoMore

> **Ras Vaughan** is at Doc Campbell's Post.
> May 29, 2017 · Instagram
>
> GET YO-YO, DAY 86 - WE WERE FEELING PRETTY BEAT DOWN ON OUR GRAND ENCHANTMENT TRAIL YO-YO ATTEMPT, when we saw this mullein which seemed to be saying, "Rock on, Ras and Kathy!"
> So rock on we must!
> What a Blessing to be Biped! Give Thanks for Life!
>
> #GETyoyo #GETit #GrandEnchantmentTrail #FeetOnTheGround #TakeLessDoMore #ZeroLimits #RunLonger #BeTrailReady #Team7hills #HShive

GET Yo-yo, Day 89 Video Transcript

West Fork Gila River: 60+ River Fords

Ras: "We are a little over ten miles deep in the West Fork of the Gila River section. There is approximately sixty crossings, six zero that is, fords of the Gila River in here, which makes it pretty challenging, logistically, in a lot of ways. It's absolutely beautiful. We've been really enjoying moving through here. And this is the section that generated the second asterisk of our yo-yo attempt where we had to deviate, due to weather, from the kind of official suggested route of the GET. So, on the second Yo, this is one of the very few sections where we have not been through before. So, it's kind of fun, that way, to be touching ground we haven't touched before. And it's amazingly beautiful in here. Further back there was a cliff dwelling off to the side. This was an area that was inhabited by the Mogollon people. And it's been really cool to just be modern Hominids moving through an ancient place where there's just been so much ancient Human activity. And being in these river cuts you can see the huge wall behind us, really unique rock formations and spires and all sorts of stuff. This is really pretty distinctive just this huge, long tall wall like this. A lot of the features have actually had more shape to them and been less just straight up and down. But, again, it's been a constantly changing environment as we wind our way along the West Fork of the Gila River."

Ras Vaughan
June 8, 2017 at 7:48pm

GET YO-YO, DAY 89 - WEST FORK GILA RIVER: 60+ RIVER FORDS
Kathy and Ras are touching this section of trail for the first time, despite this being the second yo, because the took the Highwater Bypass route on the first yo.

#GETyoyo #GETit #GrandEnchantmentTrail #FeetOnTheGround #TakeLessDoMore
#ZeroLimits #RunLonger #BeTrailReady #Team7hills #HShive

GET Yo-yo, Day 89 - West Fork Gila River: 60+ River Fords
Ras and Kathy are attempting the first known yo-yo of the Grand...
YOUTUBE.COM

Gila River Wilderness: Storms, SUNY, and the Call of the Gray Wolf

EACH MORNING WE AWOKE to the fierce heat of the southwest landscape. We stayed focused, preparing ourselves to hike for many miles. But as the morning would wear on and afternoon approached, dark and menacing clouds would build in the sky. Ras and I would keep our eye on the thunderheads, learning as each day passed, that these clouds would open up in the afternoon and pour relentlessly on us as we tried to make progress along the trail. Whether it was indeed an early monsoon season or not, we didn't really know. What we did know is that this was making it hard to continue hiking into the night as we had been doing. The rain dropping from these clouds was cold, often turning into big balls of hail. The wind would pick up as well, and Ras and I found ourselves hunkering down underneath our Six Moons Designs Gatewood Capes most afternoons. On the high ridges, the precipitation was coming in the form of snow. This spring hiking season was temperamental, and Ras and I had no choice but to continue hiking and living on the trail in these conditions.

Ras and I had made it back to Doc Campbell's Trading Post and spent the night in the RV Park, underneath a covered shelter with BBQ's and picnic tables. We picked up our resupply boxes from the wizened German storekeeper and made some purchases at his store to supplement our supplies. We both had lost a significant amount of weight. I looked downright malnourished at this point. We were very hungry. It felt good to have access to cold sodas and we both drank at least a six pack while we were there. We also paid to use the hot tub, the relaxing water coming from the natural hot springs that run through the property. The floors in the hot tub and shower house were geothermally heated. This felt like such a luxury after working so hard on the trail.

The next morning, we got our packs ready and began the three-mile road walk to the Gila River Visitor's Center, where we would meet up with the trail. We had bypassed this section on our way eastbound. Ras and I were both looking forward to hiking through this section along the Gila River. We hiked a short distance off trail, once past the visitor's center, to view some cave paintings by the Mogollon people. We took our time, not knowing whether the downpour and thunderclaps would return. They had soaked us on our road

> **Ras Vaughan** is with Kathy Vaughan at Gila River.
> June 8, 2017
>
> GET YO-YO, DAY 87 - "WHO DOES NOT REMEMBER THE INTEREST WITH WHICH, when young, he looked at shelving rocks or any approach to a cave? It was the natural yearning of that portion, any portion of our most primitive ancestor which still survived in us."
>
> -- Henry David Thoreau, Walden
>
> #GETyoyo #GETit #GrandEnchantmentTrail #FeetOnTheGround #TakeLessDoMore
> #ZeroLimits #RunLonger #BeTrailReady #Team7hills #HShive

walk towards the visitor's center, making us question whether or not we should have left Gila Hot Springs and the dry shelter we had camped underneath the night before. The rain waited until we set up an evening camp to let loose again. When morning came, we knew it was time to hustle along the 14-mile stretch of trail that forded the Middle Fork of the Gila River repeatedly.

Poison ivy bunches grew all along the banks. Ras led the way as we crossed and re-crossed the braided river. Interesting rock formations rose up, towering overhead and causing us to stop repeatedly to take in the view. We had seen an extensive cave dwelling at the trail head. It was closed off and required a guided tour to view. We were now seeing an occasional opening to a cave that looked as though ancient peoples had indeed lived there. We could see stacked rock and even old wooden framework around door openings. This was a favorite area for both Ras and I.

Right on schedule, the rain came in the afternoon as it had each day leading up to this one. We hiked on and on. The heavy rain turned to cold hail and still we pushed on, pausing to wait under huge pines in the more heavily forested areas along the route. We wanted to make progress, but considered pitching our tent in an appropriate spot, to wait out this storm. The hail stones hurt as they pummeled us. The wind whipped against our cheeks. Our capes blew and crept up our legs, making it so that we were soaked, no matter what we did to try to protect ourselves from this onslaught of precipitation.

We knew a cabin was ahead on the trail. It would likely be locked, but there might be an overhang that we could get under for some protection. Ras and I both tucked our heads down and forged on, hiking towards a cabin that we knew was up the trail somewhere. We had seen a mule train pass us at one point, each of us hunkered under our capes while the thunder clapped and the lightning bolts struck. It was a couple just a little older than us. They were probably outfitters for the forest service, we figured, or possibly even thru-hiking the Grand Enchantment Trail themselves. Who knew. We exchanged quiet hellos as we all tried to deal with the unpleasant weather conditions the best we could. The animals all looked miserable too, burdened with heavy bundles of gear.

All of a sudden, after what we thought would be the last ford of the Gila before we reached the cabin according to our trail information, we saw an empty backpacking shelter, all pitched, dry and welcoming. We heard a voice and looked up. A friendly looking guy was walking towards us and hollering over the top of the showering rain, that we were welcome to get underneath the shelter. Up ahead, underneath an identical shelter, was an entire youth group with a couple of other leaders about his age. A whole group of nearly identical tents were also set up in the area. Ras and I turned back and ran towards the shelter. What an amazing blessing to be able to get out of this rain, out here, in the middle of nowhere.

I shed my wet layers and got on some dry clothing so I could get warm. Ras and I got out our stove and began to heat up some water. After about ten minutes, the three leaders of the group came over to introduce themselves. We all hit it off right away and engaged in fun conversation, with laughter and a sense of bonding felt from our commonality of trail experiences. Ras and I shared about ourselves and our adventuring lifestyle. We offered to speak to the group after dinner if it was something they thought would be interesting. They jumped on the offer and once Ras and I had eaten our dinner, we went to

> **Ras Vaughan** is with Kathy Vaughan.
> June 8, 2017
>
> GET YO-YO, DAY 89 - HITTING THE WEST END OF THE MIDDLE FORK GILA RIVER TRAIL IN A DOWNPOUR, we found a camp of multiple tents and tarps. A friendly man stepped out and offered to let us shelter under one of their tarps. We took refuge from the storm and cooked up some food while chatting with the three leaders of what turned out to be the
> SUNY Potsdam Wilderness Education Program. They invited us to camp nearby and give an impromptu talk that evening under one of their tarp shelters as the rain pelted it.
>
> What a Blessing to meet so many like minded Hominids!
> Give Thanks for Life!
>
> #GETyoyo #GETit #GrandEnchantmentTrail #FeetOnTheGround #TakeLessDoMore
> #ZeroLimits #RunLonger #BeTrailReady #Team7hills #HShive

join the group of college aged young people gathered under the long tarp shelter.

 They had been on the trail for about ten days and for much of it they had been in rainy conditions, but they were in good spirits. They were from the State University of New York, Potsdam, and they had mainly hiked in the Adirondacks of upstate New York. The talk was casual and fun. Ras had the group cracking up repeatedly. We talked about our goal of setting an Only Known Time (OKT) on the Grand Enchantment Trail by hiking it in a yo-yo and "feet-on-the-ground" ethic, which was a new concept to most of them. We hoped to enlighten the youth to think of all the possibilities open to them. We wanted to help instill the concept that Humans are capable of amazing things, no matter where you have come from and surpassing any limits you might think you have. They asked a lot of questions. The quiet ones ended up smiling and the outspoken ones told their own stories. It was an unexpected blessing we were gifted with in the middle of the Gila National Forest.

In the morning, we departed with oatmeal and coffee as gifts. We gave everyone UltraPedestrian stickers and hugs all around. A group selfie shot was taken and off we went.

Ras and I began climbing up out of the Gila River drainage and into the Mogollon Baldy mountains.

* Day 90 6/2/17 Journal entry

Gila River, heading up to Mogollon Baldy. Life is Big; Wilderness is HUGE; My heart is enlightened; the Gila is a magnet and we can't break free from its' pull. I love it here. But we must climb high once again. The clouds are sticking around, but we must not. Miles to go=383, 19 days.*

The climb felt hard after all of the fording of the Gila from the two previous days. The fords weren't necessarily deep, but the water was rushing some and it took extra energy to push our legs through the current. I think there were about 40 fords. We reached a high shelf and followed easy singletrack through a carpet of purple and white lupine. Large bunch grasses were dry and drooping over the trail, catching my trekking poles as I hiked. The trail was quite rocky and a wildflower I had not yet seen began to show itself. Its' blossom was orange and it looked like a type of mustard.

The dark and luminous clouds finally spilled open, bringing with it loud cracks of thunder and bolts of lightning. Hail balls joined in the mix and began to pelt Ras and I relentlessly. Ras shouted to me over the storm that we had better huddle down to the ground underneath our rain capes. Luckily, before the storm had started, I had put on my Altra Zoned Heat pants. We sat on the ground with our capes over us and the storm continued with a violent and living energy. Ras and I both felt it. Water puddled up around us as we sat cross-legged. We sat quietly, waiting for enough of a break to pitch our tent so that we could crawl inside for protection. The afternoon storms had been continuing into the evening, and it was likely that this would be the end of our mileage for the day.

Ras Vaughan is with Kathy Vaughan.
June 9, 2017

GET YO-YO, DAY 90 - IT'S BEGINNING TO FEEL PERSONAL, as though New Mexico doesn't want us to complete our GET Yo-yo. Or, at least, the section of the trail between Alma and Gila Hotsprings doesn't want us to succeed. On the first Yo river and snow conditions forced us onto the High Country Bypass and High Water Bypass. And now, Westbound, on our second Yo, torrential rains with copious lightning strikes have pushed us off the trail and into our tent for the fourth day in a row. And this on what should have been a three day stretch. Perhaps the German curmudgeon at Doc. Campbell's Post was correct when he postulated that the reason no one had attempted a GET Yo-yo before was, "Because nobody is as stupid as you!" I prefer to think of us as stubborn, but not stupid. But it'll take more than the great state of New Mexico and its persistently punishing weather to foil our Grand Scheme. Although, it's sure not speeding us up any.
What a Blessing to be a Biped!
Give Thanks for Life!

#GETyoyo #GETit #GrandEnchantmentTrail #FeetOnTheGround #TakeLessDoMore
#ZeroLimits #RunLonger #BeTrailReady #Team7hills #HShive

Finally, there was enough of a break in the rain for Ras to hike ahead and scout out a flat and protected spot that would work for our tent site for the night. The flat stretch of land we were on extended for quite a distance that we could see. The Mogollon Baldy fire had swept through here so most of the trees were blackened or silvered. It was a sparse forest and a bit eerie. Ras found a good spot and came back to get me. We got the tent up and crawled inside, shivering and wet, electrified from the storm.

Changing quickly into dry layers, I felt emotional and spent. I was so glad to have this shelter. I got our sleeping bag and pads set up so we could crawl inside. Ras started the stove in the vestibule so that we could have some hot food and a drink. We felt frustrated at our slow progress due to the storms and wondered when they would abate. Ras decided to listen to the FM station on his mp3 player to see if he could get a local weather forecast. This had helped us earlier when we were caught in a snow storm and had to sleep in a culvert under the highway. When we had heard that semis were jackknifed on I40 in Albuquerque, we decided to stay put.

But now, on this quiet plateau on our way towards the summit of Mogollon Baldy, Ras was listening to oldies and I decided to get out my mp3 player and join in. We might as well have a good time while we lay comfortably in our sleeping bag, the sun now setting over the blackened forest. When a song came on that we both knew, we would sing along together. Soon, we drifted off to sleep.

I awoke, shivers going down my spine and a primal fear having swept over me. I grabbed out for Ras and he too was awake. I heard it again, a cry so unusual and wild, that it took me a minute to know what I must be hearing. We said nothing to each other, but just lay there silent. Ras looked at the time. 4:30 in the morning. It was just barely dawn. Again, we heard it, so near our tent. A Mexican Gray Wolf, lone and howling. A few minutes later, further down the trail, the cry came again. This was not a long, drawn out howl or a yipping cry like that of the coyote. This was sharp and modulating, a most unique animal call. It clearly was communicating something to us. It was not like the Mexican Gray Wolves that called back and forth to each other, off in the distance one night as Ras and I were hiking in another section of the Gila

Wilderness, earlier in our trek. This lone wolf had a message meant for Ras and I. Several more times, we heard the cry as we lay quietly. And then, no more. The wild canine was making its way along the trail, leaving its scat for Ras and I to discover the next morning. This portentous seeming night marked the end of the storms and we made it up and over Mogollon Baldy at 10,000 feet, the following day.

> **Kathy Vaughan** is with Ras Vaughan.
> June 8, 2017
>
> Evening thunderstorms have been gracing Team UltraPedestrian. We are back in Arizona with less than 2weeks to go to complete our #GETyoyo! Giving Thanks! #ZeroLimits. #TakeLessDoMore. #BeTrailReady. #HShive. #Team7Hills

GET Yo-yo, Day 93 Video Transcript

Mineral Creek Historic Mining District

Ras: "We are in Mineral Creek, outside Alma, New Mexico, in a historic mining area where there's just a lot of really cool artifacts from the time spent mining in here. Huge impact. I mean, they weren't gentle back in the day, but it's pretty impressive. This is really tough ground to cover in here. The idea of coming in here on foot 100, 150 years ago with a mule train, things like that, and then doing this sort of work is pretty freaking impressive; pouring these big concrete footers, hauling in all the pipe, hewing these timbers. This is just back breaking labor, hauling all this rock and fitting the right size pieces in. But even though this is just remains and ruins in a shambles, it's been here dealing with the weather and surviving the crazy spring floods that come through here with the snow melt for a heck of a long time. Look. Sections of this wall are still in really nice shape. Obviously from the amount of dimensional wood involved in this, they had rigged up a sawmill of some sort to pump all this out. Here's one of the locals enjoying some sun on a little piece of history. You can see more and more stacked rock off in the background. Pretty impressive. I'm always impressed with things like beaver dams, things of that sort, and it's impressive to see a similar sort of industry employed by Human Beings going after a feverish sort of goal to satisfy their lust for gold."

Ras Vaughan
June 9, 2017 at 12:57pm

GET YO-YO, DAY 93 #1 - MINERAL CREEK HISTORIC MINING DISTRICT
Kathy and Ras gawk at the backbreaking labor that went into mining operations in this area 100 years ago.

#GETyoyo #GETit #GrandEnchantmentTrail #FeetOnTheGround #TakeLessDoMore
#ZeroLimits #RunLonger #BeTrailReady #Team7hills #HShive

GET Yo-yo, Day 93, #1 - Mineral Creek Historic Mining District
Ras and Kathy are attempting the first known yo-yo of the Grand...
YOUTUBE.COM

> **Ras Vaughan** is with Kathy Vaughan.
> July 11, 2017 · YouTube
>
> THIS IS ONE OF MY VERY FAVORITE THINGS THAT HAPPENED DURING OUR GET YO-YO ATTEMPT. We were joined by two unforeseen companions as we made our way west out of Alma, New Mexico. Good thing we had these two to keep us on the straight and narrow.
>
> Give Thanks for Life!
>
> #GETyoyo #GETit #GrandEnchantmentTrail #FeetOnTheGround #TakeLessDoMore #ZeroLimits #RunLonger #BeTrailReady #Team7hills #HShive
>
> **GET Yo-yo, Day 94 - Rocking Arrow Ranch Equine Escort**
> Ras and Kathy are attempting the first known yo-yo of the Grand Enchantment Trail. Continuing on west from Alma, New Mexico, just before crossing the state l...
> YOUTUBE.COM

GET Yo-yo, Day 94 Video Transcript

Rocking Arrow Ranch Equine Escort

Ras: "We are just hiking out of Alma, New Mexico, where we had a great overnight by the San Francisco River and got to eat a bunch of treats at the Alma Store and Alma Grill where they're super kind and supportive of thru-hikers. And we're hiking out the Sunflower Mesa Road, and we just crossed onto the Rocking Arrow Ranch, and we've got an escort: these two fine equine people walking along on either side of me right now. These big beautiful horses are all white with little tiny brown speckles. One of them has a black nose, and one of them has a pink nose."

Kathy: *"They're very gentle. I just don't know what their owners are gonna think if they see them with us. I don't think they're supposed to be following us."*

Ras: *"They're wanting to stride along … oh, you wanna be scratched, huh, you wanna be scratched? You can see they're sweet. These are nice horses that obviously like people. They probably wish we had some apples or something, although I generally don't give apples to people's animals without their permission. But here we are. This is our escort across the Rocking Arrow Ranch. And, you can see, there's the Rocking Arrow brand right there. So, they've got some really beautiful ambassadors for their ranch that are escorting us across the property. Another amazing adventure as part of our Grand Enchantment Trail Yo-yo."*

* Day 95 6/7/17 Journal Entry

Dos caballos blancos followed us leaving Alma. They were friendly, people oriented and wanting attention. It was really awesome. Parched earth has surprisingly deep cracks in it. *

Kathy Vaughan
June 9, 2017

This walking stick insect with a missing feeler shows the strength and fragility of all of creation. I have seen even tinier ones. They look just like the dry desert grass. This one clamored all over the weeds and grasses as I quietly watched. I will persevere as it has, using all my strength and moving carefully until my goal is complete. After resting in the shade all day, the cool winds blow gently and urge me forward. Giving thanks for all the words of support, encouragement and understanding. #ZeroLimits #RunStronger #Team7Hills. #TakeLessDoMore. #BeTrailReady. #PureNaturalEnergy. #GETityoyo. #GrandEnchantmentTrail

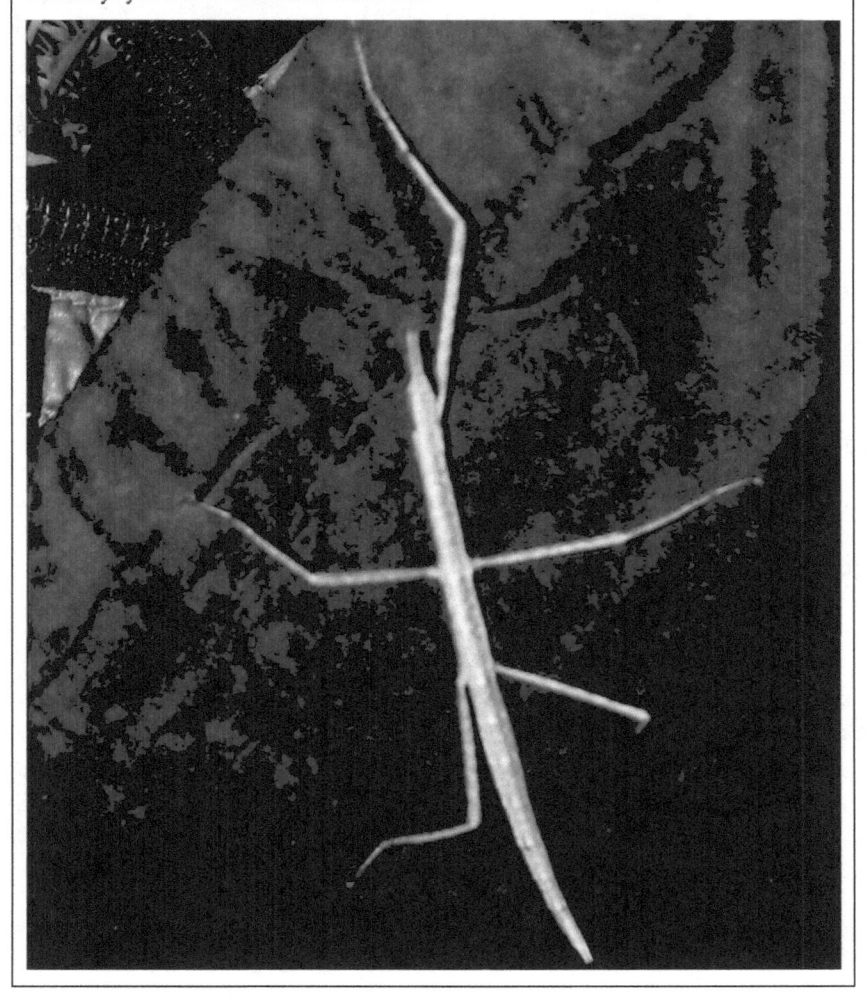

> **Ras Vaughan** is with Kathy Vaughan at Blue River (Arizona).
> June 9, 2017
>
> GET YO-YO, DAY 95 - THE ONLY THING BETTER THAN awakening in beautiful places is discovering what those beautiful places awaken in us.
>
> What a Blessing to be a Biped!
> Give Thanks for Life!
>
> #GETyoyo #GETit #GrandEnchantmentTrail #FeetOnTheGround #BackInAZ #TakeLessDoMore
> #ZeroLimits #RunLonger #BeTrailReady #Team7hills #HShive

* Day 96 6/8/17 Journal Entry

I'm sipping broth of Seoul Food seasoning, nutritional yeast, dried veggies & tomato powder to help settle my nausea. Feeling pretty yucky tonight. Ras seems tired, worn down & full of angst. He is likely stressed about water & also feeling lame about himself re: Mary not wanting him back on the crew. I feel bad for him.*

Ras Vaughan is with Kathy Vaughan at Coronado Trail.
June 9, 2017 · Clifton, AZ

GET YO-YO, DAY 97 - THE LINE BETWEEN FAILURE AND INJURY CAN BE HARD TO PERCEIVE. And after almost 100 days of struggle it's becoming difficult to balance the risk of one versus the other.

As a pancreatic disease survivor having had 40% of her pancreas removed, Kathy is more susceptible to dehydration than the average person. Since numerous rain and snow storms have repeatedly delayed us over the last three months, we are now faced with the triple digit temperatures of an Arizona June, and it is taking its toll.

Kathy's performance has been compromised over the last couple of days, and she woke up feeling queasy and low energy this morning. After only 1 1/2 miles we had to stop in the shade to wait out the heat of the day. We plan to nap until evening and then try to move through the cool of the night and make some progress toward Safford, AZ, our next resupply some 64 miles distant. For now, that is our only goal and everything else is up in the air.

We may have to zero in Safford. We may have to abandon our feet-on-the-ground ethic and hitchhike into Morenci before that for rest and recuperation. Or we may have to bail on our entire GET Yo-yo OKT project. I'm worried about Kathy's well being.

The problem with our quest to find the limits of Human Endurance is that if we succeed in so doing it will feel more like a failure than a success.

What a Blessing to be a Hominid facing such vexing question marks! Give Thanks for Life!
#GETyoyo #GETit #OneBadAssLady #GrandEnchantmentTrail
#FeetOnTheGround #TakeLessDoMore
#ZeroLimits #RunLonger #BeTrailReady #Team7hills #HShive

Ras Vaughan
June 12, 2017

GET YO-YO, DAY 98 - OUR GRAND ENCHANTMENT TRAIL YO-YO OKT ATTEMPT IS A FAIL: IT'S OVER, FINISHED, KAPUT; AND IT'S ONE OF THE GREATEST THINGS Team UltraPedestrian HAS EVER DONE. After nearly 100 days of struggle, the math and weather have turned against us so dramatically and definitively that we are left with no option but to call it quits about 40 miles shy of Safford, AZ, and approximately 300 miles short of our goal of Phoenix. Not only has the weather window of Spring slammed shut, but Summer has very suddenly made itself known with debilitating heat, making continued efforts to progress unsustainable. We tried to transition to the graveyard shift to avoid the heat, hiking through the night, but were unable to find a cool enough place to rest during the day, to the point where Kathy accidentally left her sleeping pad unattended in the direct sun for a few minutes AND IT MELTED.

Confirming our decision, when our friend Gary Housholder met up with us at the southwest end of Eagle Creek to surprise us with ice water, juice, soda, tabbouleh, hummus, veggies, apples, and a bevy of other caloric blessings, he also informed us that Mount Graham was on fire and the official GET route was closed by the Forest Service outside of Safford. Whether we wanted to accept it or not, our adventure was over.

We can (and WILL!) torture ourselves with hypotheticals about zero days we should or should not have taken, approaches we may or may not have modified, and other variables we could have potentially varied to complete our journey, but our goal was not simply to arrive at a destination, but to get there via a methodology, an ethic, a standard of comportment that we were unwilling to sacrifice, even if it endangered the entire project.

In mountaineering, this ethic is called Good Style, or Fair Means. This was expressed in our GET Yo-yo OKT attempt in our Feet-On-The-Ground ethic. Yes, if we had hitchhiked into resupply towns we could have saved time, eliminated mileage, and carried much smaller loads; meaning we could have completed the project. But it would have lacked the awkward grace and sublime brutality of covering every inch of our route on foot. To our minds, that OFF trail mileage in a vehicle would have demeaned the hundreds of thousands of footsteps we had invested ON the trail. It would have, very simply, violated our FOTG ethic. And that was never our goal. We set out to do this project in Good Style, and we never sacrificed that, even though it meant failing to reach our intended end point on the map. But Kathy and I, as Team UltraPedestrian, would rather fail according to our highest standards than succeed having sacrificed what is of importance to us. And so, alas, we have failed to complete our GET Yo-yo attempt.

I'm sure many people are wondering, and, no, we are not okay with this. It will haunt us for years to come. It will be a bugaboo prowling the periphery of our psyches for decades. We will never fully accept it. And years from now, when you see us grinding out another implausibly grueling adventure and think to yourselves, "What drives them on?" this fail will be one of the answers. And that is part of what makes it such an amazing investment. It may not have returned the immediate profits for which we had planned and hoped, but we will reap the rewards of this failure far into the future in our Life, in our Love, and in the Grand Adventure that is our time on this planet.

What a Blessing to fall short of an implausibly lofty goal! What a Blessing to be a Biped and a Hominid! What a Blessing to be a Human Being! What a Blessing to be ALIVE!

#GETyoyo #GETit #GrandEnchantmentTrail #FeetOnTheGround #TakeLessDoMore
#ZeroLimits #RunLonger #BeTrailReady #Team7hills #HShive

Kathy Vaughan is with Ras Vaughan.
June 12, 2017

There is a lightning caused fire in the Pinalenos along the #GrandEnchantmentTrail. The mountains are calling, but I must not go. Ras and I worked hard for 98 days. We hiked through places I am filled with gratitude for the chance to have experienced. I hit some of my highest highs and lowest lows. I saw creatures & features I've never seen before. I met special people & made new friends. I pushed gear to it's limits. I pushed my body & mind beyond limits I could not have imagined I would push. My love for Ras grew, despite feeling threatened at times that we could not bare the hardships any longer as partners. I drank more cow poo tea than I ever imagined I would. I felt hunger & thirst so strongly & painfully at times that I could only appreciate my American upbringing and ability to know the suffering of others in the world who cannot find relief from such emptiness on a daily. I felt the kindness of strangers and new acquaintances. I felt loneliness, and pain and joy and awe. And in the end, over 1300 miles and 98 days will have to do. Give Thanks for Life.
#ZeroLimits. #RunLonger #BeTrailReady. #TakeLessDoMore. #Team7Hills. #GETit. #PureNaturalEnergy.

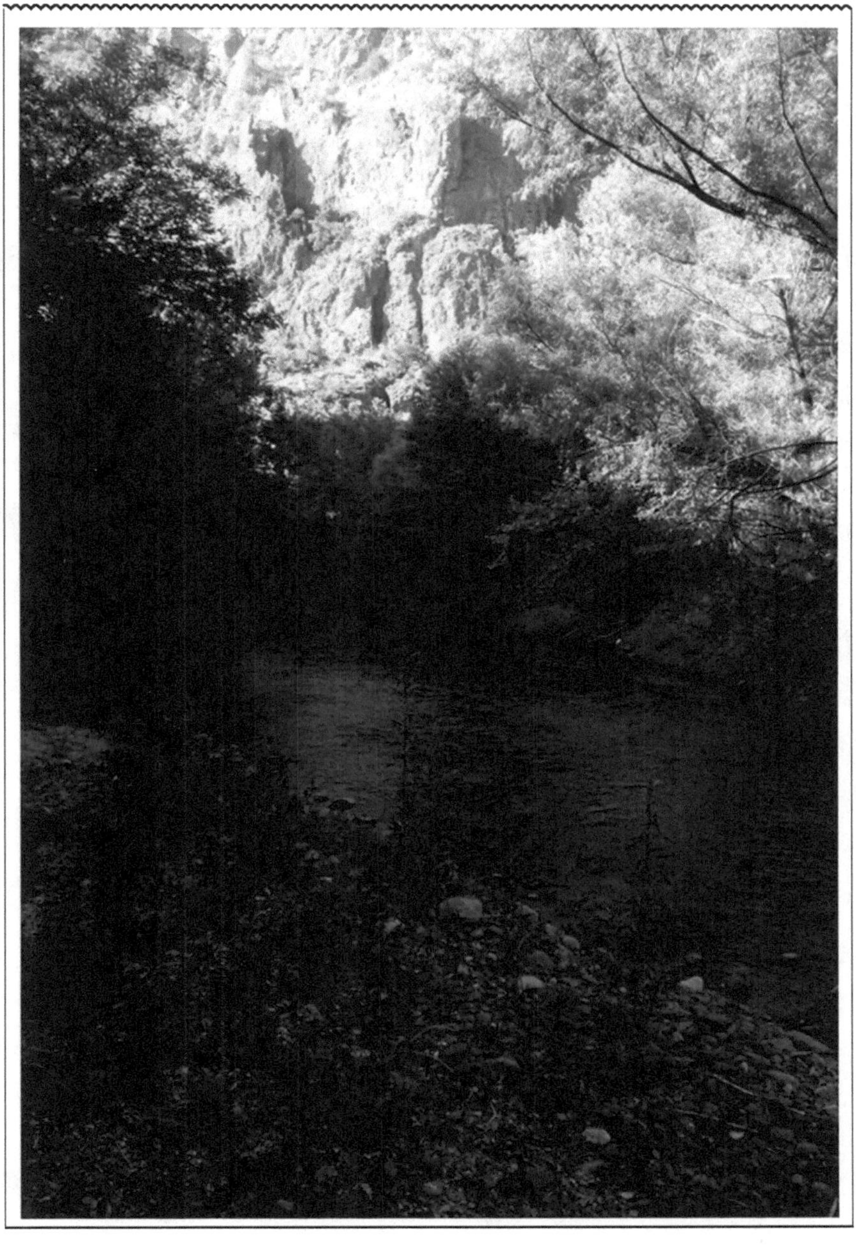

Ras Vaughan
June 11, 2017

GET YO-YO, DAY 98 - WHENEVER I DRINK FROM MY NEW TITANIUM MUG it slowly reveals a grizzled, hairy, gnomish face staring back at me from the bottom. At first I thought it was a novelty cup with the design etched into it so that it was revealed as you finish your beverage, but it turns out it's just reflective.

What a Blessing to be a not-so-well-preserved Hominid!

#GETyoyo #GETit #GrandEnchantmentTrail #FeetOnTheGround #TakeLessDoMore #ZeroLimits #RunLonger #BeTrailReady #Team7hills #HShive

Kathy Vaughan is with Ras Vaughan in 📍 Safford, Arizona.
June 13, 2017 · 🌐

'Fiya, Fiya in the mountains": Ras and I drove to Safford, AZ today to pick up some mail and 2 resupply boxes we had sent there. It is 94 degrees, we can see the smoke up in the Pinalenos where the GET continues west from where we left the trail, and Forest Service fire fighters are everywhere. It's summertime now in this area and the cotton fields have green plants now, rather than just plowed furrows. A change in seasons, a change in plans. Life continues on; it ebbs and it flows; we give and we take; acceptance and forgiveness. Give Thanks for Life! #ZeroLimits. #RunLonger. #BeTrailReady. #PureNaturalEnergy. #Team7Hills #GETit #TakeLessDoMore

Ras Vaughan is with Kathy Vaughan.
June 19, 2017

GET YO-YO ATTEMPT AFTERMATH: THE HUNGER AIN'T NO GAME. After running big daily calorie deficits for just under 100 days straight, my body and mind have shifted into a lizard brain driven survival mode, triggering an insatiable appetite. Food scarcity has dramatic effects on the Human brain, rerouting neural circuitry, increasing the proclivity toward risk taking, and affecting mood being just a few among the suite of effects. So I may not quite be myself for a while. I don't feel like myself. I don't feel like a Hominid. I feel like a shark or a velociraptor or a swarm of army ants. I feel like an eating machine. Hide the tempeh. Lock up the legumes. Secure the spinach. No calorie is safe.

What a Blessing to be Alive! Give Thanks for Life!

#GETyoyo #GETit #GrandEnchantmentTrail #FeetOnTheGround #TakeLessDoMore
#ZeroLimits #RunLonger #BeTrailReady #Team7hills #HShive

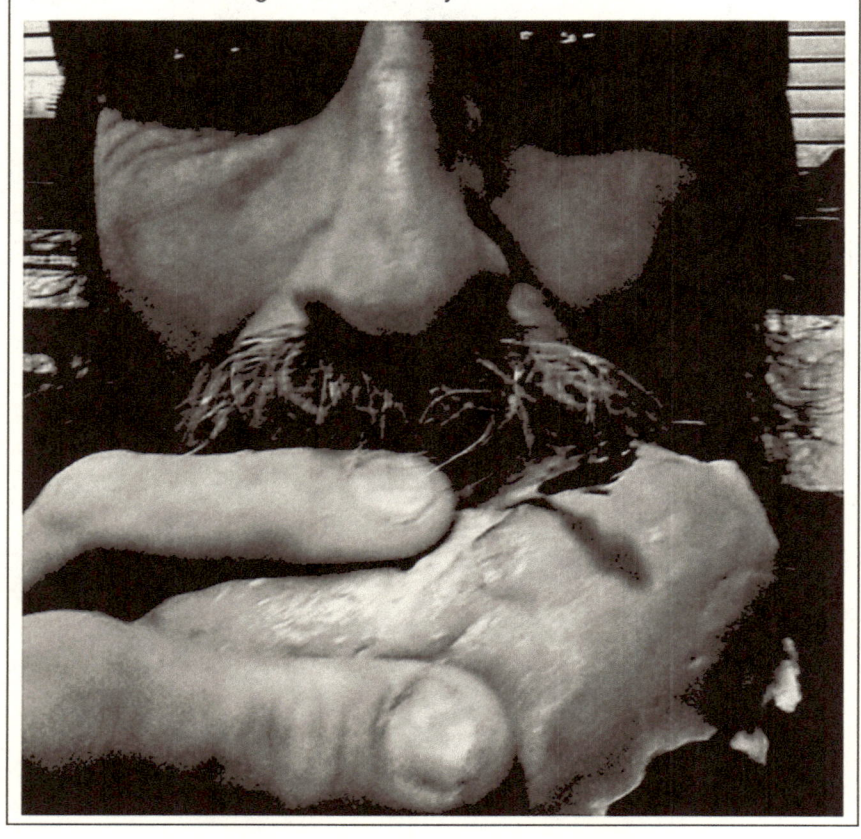

Ras Vaughan was tagged in a photo.

Kathy Vaughan is with Ras Vaughan.
July 8, 2017

My next challenge has been put before me. Ten years ago, I had my spleen and 40% of my pancreas removed after bouts of pancreatitis revealed a growth encapsulating my pancreas. I recovered and went on to become an ultrarunner, an athlete with 7 ambassadorships and completed 3 long distance thru hikes. I set a women's FKT on the first of these hikes, on the 800 mile Arizona Trail.

After returning from my most recent hike, 100 days spent on the Grand Enchantment Trail, I had some symptoms that shouted high blood sugar; unrelenting thirst and bleeding gums. These were signs that my pancreatic disease had progressed and that my pancreas was no longer producing insulin, or not enough. A blood test revealed that I am now a Type 1 Diabetic in need of 4 insulin injections each day. I will be able to continue with my endurance sports lifestyle, learning how to bring my injection kit along with me on the trail. Ras is my rock and has been by my side with support, drilling the docs and pharmacist and helping to ensure that Team UltraPedestrian continues to kick ass. #OBALunbranded. #ZeroLimits. #RunLonger. #BeTrailReady. ##TakeLessDoMore. #Team7Hills. #PureNaturalEnergy

98 DAYS OF WIND

Ras Vaughan is with Kathy Vaughan.
July 10, 2017

REGARDLESS OF WHAT THE UNIVERSE AND/OR FATE AND/OR CHANCE THROWS AT US, Team UltraPedestrian is up to the challenge. Always improving, constantly progressing. Infinite energy, unlimited potential. Purely positive. Forwards ever, backwards never.

Give Thanks for Life!

#OneBadAssLady #TypeOneBadAss #ZeroLimits #RunLonger #TakeLessDoMore #BeTrailReady #Team7hills #HShive

The Grand Enchantment Fail, A Diagnoses, and Life Beyond

I SPIT THE TOOTHPASTE MIXED WITH BLOOD out of my mouth and then I spit again. Each time I tried to rid my mouth of the blood, I would just spit more. I figured that after a couple of months on the trail with not enough attention paid to oral hygiene, I might be experiencing some gum issues. I spit again, and more blood spewed out. It seemed like an unusual amount.

Little did I know my pancreas had stopped producing insulin and I had become a Type 1 Diabetic. My blood sugar levels were very high, dangerously so. Bleeding gums was only one of the symptoms I had been experiencing. My vision had become blurry, but since most of my time was spent hiking, I hadn't tried to read anything in weeks. I did not realize how my vision had deteriorated as the sugars flowed through my blood stream, causing it to change even the lenses of my eyes.

My thirst was out of control. I could not quench it, no matter what or how much I drank. I was not surprised that during a long desert thru-hike my thirst would be so intense. With these three symptoms being classic signs of diabetes, had I had access to Google, I would have probably known I was diabetic months before my diagnosis.

I had been hiking with Ras since March fourth. We were nearly 1,300 miles into a thru-hike yo-yo of the Grand Enchantment Trail. We were just 300 miles shy of completing our journey, a goal we had been working very hard towards achieving. I was feeling relentless nausea. I had become quite thin. The heat was becoming intense as we got further west, closing in on Phoenix and the Sonoron Desert. Ras and I didn't understand the entirety of what was going on with my health. We attributed everything to the hike and the physical and mental toll it was taking on both of us.

We had been hiking about 20 miles every day since we began from Phoenix in March. We hiked from after our breakfast and morning routine, until between 11 and midnight. We stopped for breaks, filtering water, and shade-time if needed, but for the most part, we were hiking. The terrain was not easy, by any means. The Grand Enchantment Trail is an East/West Route that begins (or ends) in Phoenix, Arizona and travels through deserts, washes, sky islands and mountain ranges, as well as forests to reach Albuquerque, New Mexico, in 740 miles. The trail is very remote, and the resupply options are few and far between. Hikers either begin in Phoenix in the Spring and hike towards Albuquerque, or they begin in Albuquerque in the Fall and hike to Phoenix. No one has ever hiked the trail both directions in one push, and that is what Ras and I had intended to do. We set an Only Known Time for this on the Arizona National Scenic Trail and our goal was to complete it on the GET as well.

But the universe had other plans for us. Our hike was an adventure from the beginning. We welcomed it with open arms, though. I journaled through the highs and lows of it all. Ras navigated through all the varying types of terrain, following the GPS and setting forth a daily goal for us, based on water sources, places to camp and what lay ahead on the trail.

We hiked in snow pack and had fresh snow fall come down on us. We hiked through canyons, working our way along creek drainages filled with ice cold snow melt. We traveled endless miles on dirt roads. We camped amongst cow pies and drank water from their water tanks. We also shared a water source with a young cougar. We saw wild turkey, horned toads, black widows, Big Horn Desert Sheep, a baby rattler, elk with impressive racks, fish in the streams and scorpions in the washes.

Epilogue

There is nowhere that Ras and I would rather be than on the trails together. We have worked for nearly 5 years to make this happen, full-time, for ourselves. Completing this thru-hike was going to be a step in the right direction for us in achieving this goal. We had sponsorship help from Nathan and Altra Running. We had Trail Butter pouches and Honey Stinger waffles. We had tons of ultra-light backpacking gear from Gossamer Gear, including our trekking poles, the Deuce of Spades, Ras' pack, our ¾ length sleeping pads and cuben fiber gear bags.

But the heat and the nausea and the bleeding gums and the weight loss wouldn't let up. My final night of hiking, I had a meltdown. I cried and panicked and wondered how I could go on, but also, how I could stop. It was rough and ugly. Ras and I stopped for a break on some flat rocks, the full moon casting its glow down on us. The tears wouldn't stop coming. Ras had no comfort for me; it had to come from myself and I couldn't muster any. From behind us, echoing off the jagged cliffs, an eerie cry resounded in the otherwise quiet night. Ras suggested I listen to a book and that the carefully crafted words could pull me out of my funk. I resisted at first, but finally settled on listening to a book I had already listened to many times on this hike, "Pioneer Grit". This was a story about a number of strong pioneer women who had overcome amazing adversity. It was just what I needed. I spoke not a word, but listened for hours into the night. The trail was exceptionally challenging with route finding, overgrown brush, downed trees, narrow trail and a sense of being never-ending. It was one of the harder nights I've experienced.

At dawn, Ras filtered water from a dank spring, while Harvestman spiders crawled from the old cottonwood trees that lined the water source. I ate something, I don't remember what. Ras and I were still silent with each other. It was a dark time. We continued on the trail with our water bottles full now. The sky continued to lighten, and it felt good to have covered some miles in the night. We had another canyon to work our way through before we got to Eagle Creek, where we had over 40 fords awaiting us. Beyond the creek, our friend Gary Householder planned on meeting us with fresh food and water, and in the back of our minds, we knew this would be a way to get off the trail if we so decided. This canyon was rugged and scenic, mysterious piles of horse poop led the way, and something dead created an overpowering stench and a feast for a half-dozen vultures.

When we reached Eagle Creek, I thought our plan was to find some shade and pitch our tent to sleep. We had hiked all through the night, and now it was time to have a proper meal and rest. Ras had other plans. He wanted to find a really nice shade spot, but only after covering a couple more hours of hiking. I didn't have it in me without a meal. I had come through that middle-of-the-night meltdown and now I felt another one coming on. I was so hungry. I could not believe we were this far off on our needs and plans. I tried to hold it together, but to no avail. I broke down once again,

Ras could now see that I indeed needed to address some of my needs and so we found a decent place to set up our camp alongside Eagle Creek. We had 14 miles and the 40 fords in the warm, cow impacted water, before we reached the spot where Gary planned to meet us that night. We had enough time to eat and nap. But it was hot, triple digit hot. We ate and crawled into our tent, lying just on our sleeping pads. We didn't even bother to get out our sleeping bag, knowing there was no way we would need it. We fell asleep immediately.

I awoke in a pool of sweat. It felt awful. I didn't want to wake Ras up, but I had to get out of the tent and get to the creek. I had to wet myself down. It felt so good to take a dip, get my hair wet and wet down my bandana to put over my forehead when I went back to the tent to try to catch some more sleep. In the time I was gone, my sleeping pad had been exposed to the hot sun and warped. I could not believe it. Ras began to stir. He looked at me and said, "I'm worried about you."

Epilogue

We went back down to the creek and began to soak in the water. It wasn't the most refreshing water, but it was there, and it saved us from the stifling heat. The sound of the rapids was soothing. Ras and I looked at each other and tears began to stream down our cheeks. We knew. We could not hike 300 more miles in these conditions, with my mental and physical health having deteriorated, and the sun melting our gear before our very eyes. (It has taken me five months to even write this, and I'm crying now as I type.) This was hard.

When Gary met us late that night, he informed us of a forest fire forcing closure of the GET beyond Safford, several days of hiking ahead of us. Indeed, our hike was over, and the Grand Enchantment Trail Yo-yo attempt was coming to a close after 98 days and 1,300 miles.

After picking up resupply boxes we had shipped ahead, visiting with our southwest friends, and driving the long stretch from Arizona back to Washington, I finally got in to see a doctor. My A1C was above 14, a number that was immeasurable. I was diagnosed as a Type 1 Diabetic at that appointment and given the myriad prescriptions needed to begin insulin therapy. I weighed 106 pounds. I had been peeing out all the glucose and nutrients my body so desperately needed to survive, let alone hike in challenging terrain day after day. So many questions were now answered, and so many new ones had now arisen.

Fast forward to five months down the road. For three months, Ras and I spent the summer together getting out on some weekend adventures. I started back with the weeding service I worked for right away, having accumulated some debt during our thru-hike and needing to get started on repaying that. Plus, I was hungry and thirsty and I wanted some cash flow to get nutrients in myself and Ras. Needless to say, after being on insulin, which is a weight gain hormone, and having the luxury to satisfy my nutrient needs and cravings, I have gotten back up to a healthy weight. My A1C was down to 9.2 at my last appointment, and my daily readings are almost always in range. I am getting used to this and I am beyond ready to get out on another extended hike.

My biggest accomplishment post-diagnosis, was to summit Mt. Adams, a 12,000 foot volcano in the Cascade Mountain Range of Washington. It was amazing. I now want to climb Mt. St. Helens, Glacier Peak and Mt. Rainier in the Cascades as well. I felt so strong and did well in the high elevations. Ras and I did this together to celebrate my 51st birthday. It was challenging to ascend the steep and rocky North Cleaver. We traversed the summit and descended the South Spur route, steep snowfields all the way to the base. We then had a 25k run back to our car. It was the highlight of my summer.

The summer ended with Ras traveling to South Africa, where he was able to complete the Drakensburg Grand Traverse through the Maloti Mountains of Lesotho. He then continued on to Madagascar to visit our daughter, who is serving in the Peace Corps there. He will be putting together a photo book to document his travels in Madagascar.

I spent the remainder of the summer continuing my yard work job with Mary's Weeding Service and spending as much time as possible on the local trails, as I continued to adjust to my insulin therapy. I am blessed to live only a short distance away from a wonderful network of trails in the Fort Ebey, South Whidbey and Deception Pass State Parks. I stopped at one of these parks on my way home from work each day to run for an hour or two. These miles were for maintaining fitness, creating space for mindfulness each day, and pondering what path my life was taking. To live a healthy life as a diabetic, I need to continue to prioritize these times on the trail, whether I find myself alone while Ras pursues other adventures, teamed up with him, or partnered with other adventurers. I will continue living a life of inner and outer exploration.

Magdalena May, More Than Worth Her Weight

HER EYES STARED BLANKLY AT ME from where she sat atop the shelf just inside the closed Gila River National Visitor's Center. I could tell right away that she was soft, plush, and sweet. She was waiting to be nurtured, held close and loved. Her coat was mottled gray, with a tuft of wiry looking hair between her pointy ears. Her snout had a beige tip, and her short legs had small, cloven hoofs at their ends. She was adorable and I couldn't stop thinking about her as I hiked away from the building. It would be 800 miles of hiking, at an intensity and level of excitement that I never could have predicted, before I would see this face again; this stout, yet soft-seeming, stuffed javelina.

When I was a child, I had asthma and it would often be worse at night. I discovered that if I propped my big stuffed turtle underneath my head, it would silence the rattling in my chest, what sounded to me like little voices chit chatting away and making it hard for me to breathe. My sister and I would play stuffed animal games before falling asleep each night, and my brother would call out from his bedroom, trying to join in the games. I outgrew the asthma and the stuffed animal games, but the comfort and playfulness that these soft toy animals induce has stuck with me. During a long thru-hike, while spending chunks of time away from my pets, my soul longs for critters to nurture. I find myself talking to the squirrels, the kangaroo rats, the horned toads, jack rabbits and even a Sonoran Desert tortoise on one occasion.

It is not unusual for thru-hikers to carry a trail buddy with them. I sew small trail totem dolls from recycled fabrics, stuffing them with wool and adorning them with outfits and style. I have gifted trail friends and family with these dolls, although I do not carry one myself. Ras gave me a small tortoise named Cruiser just before our last hike, and Cruiser joined me on the Grand Enchantment Trail in Arizona and New Mexico.

I loved having Cruiser with me. I stuffed him inside my pack so I wouldn't lose him and I tried hard to keep him clean. He was bright green with tan markings and had huge eyes. Sometimes, I would take him out of my pack to take pictures of him in especially scenic settings. Then I would zip him right back into the Gossamer Gear cuben fiber pouch where he lived, with my pinon sap, salve, journal and other special trail items.

One morning, Ras and I spent quite a bit of time in camp drying out our gear in the sunshine. We had been caught in a snow storm in the Manzano Mountains the day before. As we descended to this drive-up camp, lonely this time of year, the snow turned to rain. We holed up inside an outhouse to dry off, until we discovered a black widow in her web high in the corner of the small space. Ras braved the weather to set up our tent and we slept soundly in the dry space. Two rangers drove into the camp the next morning to fill up their water tank, and Ras struck up a conversation with them. I basked in the warm sunshine and set Cruiser in a grassy spot to take a couple of pictures. I became distracted by trying to eavesdrop on the conversation, and soon forgot all about little Cruiser.

Sometime later that morning, hiking swiftly downhill, I thought of him, sitting in the grass. I cried out without even realizing it, "Oh Cruiser!" My insides sank and my heart felt immediately heavy as the vague wondering of whether I might have accidentally left him there turned into the strong reality that I most certainly had.

Ras heard me cry out and knew what had happened. He felt so bad for me and patiently allowed me to mourn the loss of a little stuffed animal, a trail friend. The small tortoise had been with me for nearly 1,000 miles. I got a little lift each time I saw those goofy big eyes. I could not believe the heart ache I felt upon leaving this guy behind, or the sadness I would feel as I thought of him alone there in the grass, next to the fence in the empty campground.

Days later, sopping wet from a deluge and the wrath of a desert thunder storm, Ras and I sat outside the now open Gila National Visitor's Center. We were on the return Yo of our yo-yo attempt on the Grand Enchantment Trail. We pulled off our dripping capes and found a place to hang them to dry. I stripped off a couple of other layers and made myself presentable. It was time to go inside and warm up, check out the displays, and maybe see if a shy, plush, stuffed javelina still lived here.

I am drawn to hiking in the desert, due in part to having spent my life in the Pacific Northwest. The desert is mysterious and special, hosting wildlife, plants and terrain that is all new to me. I have thru-hiked the 800 mile Arizona National Scenic Trail, yo-yoed that same trail, and hiked 1,300 miles of the Grand Enchantment Trail in a yo-yo attempt during the spring of 2017. During these hikes, I have been able to both see and hear the little wild pigs called javelinas. The first experience I had with them, I heard the snorting and grunting before I saw the dark and wiry creatures. There were a couple of them together rooting around in the dry, cattle impacted zone around the Gila River. The second sighting was during my yo-yo hike of the AZT with Ras in the fall of 2016. Ras and I were joined for 100 miles by my friend Lisa Eversgerd. We had hiked off the trail to investigate the possibility of filtering water from the Gila, and as we approached the banks of the river, a limping javelina came towards Lisa and I. I screeched as I leapt towards her, not being familiar with the animal, and hearing stories of their vicious tendencies. This guy had no desires to harm us and really just seemed a little down on its luck, limping and all. I felt bad for it as we watched it hobble away.

My third sighting of javelinas was during my GET hike, wandering along the scenic rocks of the Slickrock Wonderland in New Mexico. Ras and I both felt the presence of other beings, and soon saw a small pack of javelinas. One stood out from the others and I assumed it was a mother. This one was not dark and wiry looking, but instead was mottled gray.

Ras and I wandered the inside of the Visitor's Center, looking at the displays of the early Mogollon peoples that had lived along the Gila. We spent an hour inside, at least, and finally came to the shelves where the stuffed animals were. Other animals that represented images and memories we had shared along the trail were there, but the longing eyes and soft fur of the javelina I had seen 800 miles and a myriad of experiences previously, left me but no choice. I named her Magdalena May (after my favorite trail town, Magdalena, NM and it being the month of May) and found a place for her at the top of my already plump pack, having just picked up a resupply in the small community of Gila Hot Springs. She would be my pillow and my companion, not to mention a way to fill the hole in my heart that had been made when I left Cruiser behind.

It was ridiculous. She's big, not a small, reasonable sized trail totem. But Ras insisted, and I'm glad he did. Yes, I'm 51 and entirely too old to play with stuffed animals. A thru-hike is life changing, intense, beautiful, impactful and teaches us to tap into our Inner Hominid. I thrive on the trails, whether it is my daily run or cross-country ski trip, or when I am out on a multi-month adventure hike. It's my essence, my core, my call. While out there, I am content. An inanimate object that can absorb my tears of joy or pain; ride along in my pack just for the pleasure of it; prop my head up at night; cause me to laugh or talk silly or share a goofy moment with Ras; and helps instill in me the belief that it serves as my guidance and protection on the trail, she's worth more than her weight.

Kathy's Gear List

Backpack
Nathan Journey Fastpack

Sleeping System
Gossamer Gear Nightlight Sleeping Pad

Kitchen
Titanium cup & spork

Water System
Nathan Fire & Ice 2 750 ml Hydration Bottle x 2

First Aid/Hygiene/Repair
Cheap collapsible toothbrush
Sample size tube of toothpaste
Bandana x 2
Hairbrush and hair ties
Chemical handwarmers
Lighter
Toilet paper
Sunscreen
Lip balm

Clothes
Altra performance skirt
Altra T-shirt
Altra buff
Smartwool buff
Trail Butter "Be Trail Ready" trucker cap
Cheap fleece jacket
Synthetic earflap hat
Smartwool armsleeves
Eddie Bauer puffy vest
Snowboarding gloves
Knee high wool socks
Injinji midweight socks x 2 pairs
Thigh high wool socks
Montbell puffy pants

Mountain Hardwear puffy jacket
Altra Lone Peak 3.0 shoes/Altra Lone Peak NeoShell 3.0 Insulated shoes
Altra Trail Gaiters
Altra Zoned Heat pants
Six Moon Designs Gatewood Cape

Electronics
BLU smartphone
Sony Walkman mp3 player

Miscellaneous
Black Diamond Polar Icon headlamp
Gossamer Gear LT4S CARBON TREKKING POLE
Gossamer Gear Cuben Q-Storage Sacks x 2
Gossamer Gear LITEFLEX HIKING (CHROME) umbrella

Ras' Gear List

Backpack
Gossamer Gear Mariposa 60 (switched packs halfway through)
Gossamer Gear Walker 75 (prototype)
Nathan Firestorm Running Vest rigged as a front pack

Shelter
Six Moons Designs Haven Net Tent & Tarp
Tarptent Saddle Two (switched to Tarptent halfway through)

Sleeping System
Feathered Friends Penguin Nano 20 down bag with Penguin Groundsheet for use as a two-person quilt with bottom sheet
Gossamer Gear Nightlight Sleeping Pad

Kitchen
Jetboil Flash Cooking System
Cheap plastic container with watertight lid
Snowpeak titanium spork

Water System
Sawyer Squeeze Filter
Nathan 2 liter bladders x 4 = 2 for dirty 2 for clean
Nathan Flexshot 1 liter x 2
Nathan Fire & Ice 2 750 ml Hydration Bottle x 2

First Aid/Hygiene/Repair
Cheap collapsible toothbrush
Sample size tube of toothpaste
Bandana
Toenail clippers
Leather sewing needles x 3
Upholstery thread - 1 spool
Superglue
12' duct tape
Tenacious Tape precut patches
Tenacious Tape roll
Chemical handwarmers - 1 pack for emergency
Lighter
Toilet paper
Sunscreen - stick type

Clothes
Altra running shorts - 1 pair
Cheap long sleeve button up shirt
Synthetic buff
Trail Butter "Be Trail Ready" trucker cap
Cheap fleece hat
Synthetic earflap hat
Smartwool armsleeves
Zensah wool calf sleeves
Black Diamond mountaineering gloves
Zensah lightweight gloves
Injinji midweight socks x 2 pairs
Injini lightweight wool socks, 1 pair
Smartwool midweight socks
Western Mountaineering puffy pants
Mont Bell synthetic puffy
Western Mountaineering ultralight puffy
Altra Lone Peak shoes/Altra Lone Peak NeoShell Insulated shoes
Altra Trail Gaiters

Homemade Puffy Down Slippers made from the sleeves off an old down coat
Six Moon Designs Gatewood Cape

Electronics
Nokia 930 Windows Phone
Garmin eTrex 20 handheld GPS
24000 mAh battery pack/charger
Sony Walkman mp3 player
SPOT Gen 1 Satellite Transponder
GoPro Hero 3+ Silver edition

Miscellaneous
Black Diamond Polar Icon headlamp
Gossamer Gear LT4S CARBON TREKKING POLE
Gossamer Gear Cuben Q-Storage Sacks x 3
Gossamer Gear STICKPIC SELFIE ADAPTER
Gossamer Gear LITEFLEX HIKING (CHROME) UMBRELLA
Gossamer Gear Pack Liner

Acknowledgments

Our adventures would not be possible without the love and support of our family and friends. Thank you for your encouragement as we pursue our dreams and follow our own path, even though frequently has us far away and incommunicado.

Thank you to all of our supporters around the world who follow our adventures and share the UltraPedestrian ethos. Knowing that so many of you are vicariously accompanying us on our journeys as well as pursuing your own adventures helps keep us moving forward during the challenging times. Your comments and encouragement are a vital part of the Circle of Mutual Inspiration.

Thanks also to our sponsors, without whose assistance these projects would be impossible. Special thanks to Altra Running, who has shared and supported the UltraPedestrian vision from the beginning. Thanks also to Gossamer Gear, Nathan Sports, Injinji Toesocks, Trail Butter, Seven Hills Running Shop, and Honey Stinger.

Finally, thank you to a special supporter whom we know would prefer to remain nameless. Your generosity has been indispensable to our quest to find the limits of Human endurance.

Resources

For up to date information about the Grand Enchantment Trail, including the official website and access to all of Ras & Kathy's video trail dispatches from the GET Yo-yo attempt, please visit:

UltraPedestrian.com/get